ANARCHY AND THE
SEX QUESTION

ESSAYS ON WOMEN AND

EMANCIPATION, 1896–1926

Revolutionary Pocketbooks

ANARCHY AND THE SEX QUESTION

ESSAYS ON WOMEN AND
EMANCIPATION, 1896–1926

Emma Goldman
Edited by Shawn P. Wilbur

Anarchy and the Sex Question: Essays on Women and Emancipation, 1896–1926
Emma Goldman
Editor: Shawn P. Wilbur
This edition copyright © 2016 PM Press
All rights reserved. No part of this book may be transmitted by any
means without permission in writing from the publisher.

ISBN: 978-1-62963-144-8
Library of Congress Control Number: 2016930992

Cover by John Yates/Stealworks
Layout by Jonathan Rowland based on work by briandesign

10 9 8 7 6 5 4 3 2 1

PM Press
PO Box 23912
Oakland, CA 94623
www.pmpress.org

Printed in the USA by the Employee Owners of Thomson-Shore in
Dexter, Michigan. www.thomsonshore.com

■ CONTENTS

■ "LET US NOT OVERLOOK VITAL THINGS"

A FEW WORDS OF INTRODUCTION
Shawn P. Wilbur

Even anarchists have their "names to conjure with," and among those the name of Emma Goldman must occupy a special place. It has grown fashionable in some circles to claim, as Margaret C. Anderson once did, that "Emma Goldman's genius is not so much that she is a great thinker as that she is a great woman," but if that was true, in some sense at least, it was not because she lacked genius. Anderson's observation that "she preaches, but she is a better artist than she is a preacher" brings us close to a truth about the power of Goldman's written works, which have remained of interest to successive generations of readers—to a degree that may be unmatched in the anarchist literature. Renowned as a speaker, Goldman also wrote with a remarkable directness and immediacy. Indeed, if Anderson's account is to be believed, perhaps Goldman the artist was even more successful on the printed page than at the podium. Having attended a series of Goldman's lectures in Chicago, Anderson observed that "with the exception of two or three lectures she didn't get away from the obvious sufficiently to make the series distinctive." Let those who are so inclined argue about whether Goldman's essays are *profound*, according to their own chosen standards, but history seems to attest that they continue to be *interesting*.

They continue to be influential as well, with *Anarchism and Other Essays* remaining one of the most frequently recommended introductions to anarchism, over a hundred years after its first publication, and no doubt the primacy of art over preaching has contributed to the comparative timelessness of the works. The literary qualities of the essays should come as no surprise to us, given the prominent place of art and literature in Goldman's speeches and writings, and indeed throughout the pages of *Mother Earth*. But there is another aspect of Goldman's thought that has undoubtedly tended to lift her work above the various, and often very specific, contexts in which it was originally written: an individualism influenced by figures like Friedrich Nietzsche and Max Stirner. Whatever the subject of the essays, Goldman herself appears as a powerful presence in the work, exhorting and conjuring, full of powerful enthusiasms and disillusionments. "Let us be broad and big," she wrote in "The Tragedy of Woman's Emancipation." "Let us not overlook vital things, because of the bulk of trifles confronting us." However distant or even "trifling" we may now find the occasions for Goldman's essays, her focus on the "broad and big," the boldness of her expression and her own individual vitality tend to lend them an air of immediacy and significance..

To truly do justice to all that is vital in Goldman's work, it is necessary to recognize her breadth, to engage with her as both preacher and artist, and to recognize the real distance that often separates us from her. We have to take care not let Goldman's great vitality of style distract us from vital facts and distinctions, or from potentially important shifts and even confusions Immediacy can, after all, be something of a double-edged sword, and polemics aimed at specific historical moments may require closer and closer examination as that moment recedes into the past. Connecting with what was vital for our predecessors often demands a certain broadness and bigness on our part, a willingness to at least temporarily set aside what seems most vital to us.

Given these cautions, one might reasonably ask: Why yet *another* Emma Goldman collection? Why these texts? Why now? Why, particularly, if it appears they present us with an illusion of immediacy, seeming to speak about things that are important to us? The answers to those questions take us back to the realm of conjuration—both conjuring up and conjuring away—and the specific circumstances under which this collection was conceived.

———

I was reminded of that phrase, "a name to conjure with," a couple of years ago, while making the rounds of the summer book fairs. I had become very interested in the women active in the early French socialist movement and had begun to translate some previously untranslated texts into English. I assembled two issues of a pamphlet with the *descriptive* if not exactly *elegant* title *Black and Red Feminism from Nineteenth Century France*. They included essays, poems, and bits of short fiction by and about writers like Jeanne Deroin, Jenny P. d'Héricourt, Victoire Léodile Béra (André Léo), Flora Tristan, and Paule Mink.

The reception was, unsurprisingly, a bit tepid. Those are not exactly household names. Tristan is remembered for her proto-syndicalist proposal for a Workers' Union. Béra and Mink figure as minor characters in the story of the Paris Commune. Deroin and d'Héricourt are sometimes recalled as women with whom Proudhon debated. But all had the misfortune to have been most active in the period before the First International, to have been most closely associated with socialist currents we now tend to consider "utopian," and to have written works that were as literary as they were political. While their radicalism hardly fits the familiar narrative of "first-wave" feminism, its form has not been easy to situate in other sorts of radical history.

That said, while I had anticipated quite a range of reasons why these writings might face resistance from modern readers, the implied disapproval of Emma Goldman was one response I had not expected. But on several different occasions browsers looked up from the *Black and Red Feminism* pamphlets to declare, with no other prompting, that "Emma Goldman was not a feminist."

There are statements that are true but still raise more questions than they answer. This invocation of Goldman against other radical women seemed to be of that class, but as the response came, unbidden, again and again, it became clear that there is something in Emma Goldman's attitude towards "feminism"—or our present perception of that attitude—that resonates for at least parts of the anarchist movement, and in ways that raise yet another obstacle to our appreciation of some early radical women. As a result, it became important to know in what senses Emma Goldman either was or was not a "feminist" and then to know whether this identification was a "vital thing" or a "trifle" with regard to Goldman's own thought. Lacking immediate answers, I relaunched the pamphlet series as *La Frondeuse: Unruly Writing by Radical Women*, and this more *elegant*, but not exactly *descriptive* alternative has served me at least as well as the original, although recovering this lost history—however we want to label it—remains a difficult task.* Then I set to work gathering and examining Goldman's writings on what she herself called "the sex question."

The major works are, for the most part, well known, if not, perhaps, entirely understood. Assembling them was quick work and they appeared together as the third of the new *La Frondeuse* pamphlets. The next time the specter of Emma Goldman was conjured up in response to one of my historical projects, I was simply able to hand the critic the collection and let them decide for themselves whether Goldman was a "feminist" and in what sense it mattered. Then, almost immediately, I was asked to transform that bundle of texts into book form, and there was no delaying a more exhaustive search and at least some provisional answers of my own.

I began this long aside by suggesting that Goldman's own vitality, her skills as a preacher, may sometimes distract us

---

* The title was inspired by a collection of sketches by Séverine (Caroline Rémy de Guebhard) and the French feminist newspaper *La Fronde*. A *frondeuse* is literally a woman wielding a sling, and figuratively a trouble-maker or giant-killer. The current project archive can be found at http://lafrondeuse.org.

from the vital details in her various works.. But we also have to ask if there is something in us—or in our context—that makes strong declarations for or against identifications like "feminism" so appealing that we may be inclined to respond to Goldman the artist as if she were instead a preacher. What seems clear is that the question of "feminism" is indeed significant for us, so it makes sense to address it first, in order to move on to a more direct engagement with Goldman's "sex question."

———

We know that Emma Goldman was, in fact, a critic of "feminism" in at least some sense. On March 14, 1915, for example, she was scheduled to give a talk on "Feminism—A Criticism of Woman's Struggle for the Vote and 'Freedom.'" She gave some version of the talk on numerous occasions. When she spoke in San Francisco, on July 9 of the same year, the title was amended to "The Follies of Feminism." She obviously took some pleasure in the confrontations that resulted. Regarding a speech on "Feminism" at the Woman's City Club in Los Angeles, she wrote:

> 500 woman-rights women, from the deepest red to the dullest gray came to see and hear the "disreputable" Emma Goldman. Once in the lions' den, I decided if I was to be devoured I must arouse the appetite of the beast to its right proportion. Was it the impudence on my part, or that the City Club women are a tame set? In any event, I am still alive, skin and all.

Following the San Francisco appearance, David Leigh reported:

> "The Follies of Feminism" brought out a troop of the faith-charged. It was written in their eyes that they believed heaven itself attainable if only decision be inscribed and dropped in a box. The hall was dotted with unconscious surprises when Miss Goldman told how the women of

Colorado were the ones who had fought Ben Lindsley the hardest when he had sought via the polls to render further service to his fellowmen. She drew a life portrait of that police person, Katie Davis, showing how delicate the gentle sex is when it gets a first-rate chance to sandpaper the feelings of helpless humanity. Somehow the opinions that went out of the hall were different from those which came in. It does our sisters good to hear the truth about themselves; and to hear what a useless little plaything voting-paper is.

But this was clearly not the whole story. What Goldman lamented in her 1906 essay "The Tragedy of Woman's Emancipation" was, after all, not the struggle for liberation but the "disgraceful degeneration" of that struggle. As she put it, "woman is confronted with the necessity of emancipation from emancipation, if she really desires to be free." In order to understand the vehemence of Goldman's condemnation, we have to understand what it is that she found particular "disgraceful" about suffragists and feminists, starting with the lack of "spirit, fire, and idealism." Unsurprisingly, it was a question of sex and of vitality.

"Emancipation from emancipation" was a project that left its participants considerable leeway where language was concerned. The French *frondeuses* and *éclaireuses* found new labels to distinguish themselves from others associated with "feminism." Charlotte Perkins Gilman promoted a "larger feminism," while criticizing the smallness of existing forms, and inspired Floyd Dell to include Goldman among the representative figures of "modern feminism" in his 1913 study, *Women as World Builders*. Others, such as Dora Marsden and Nelly Roussel, used the term Goldman rejected to designate something very much like the revolution she proposed. Roussel, recognizing the controversy over the "badly understood and falsely interpreted" term, was "not afraid to assert that some men, and many women, are 'feminists' without knowing it, all while rejecting the title."

Even the pages of *Mother Earth* sometimes contained an enthusiastic mention of "feminism," without contradicting Goldman's position in any significant way. In August 1915, while Goldman was out speaking on its follies, Max Baginski's "Observations and Comments" contained a review of a pamphlet on "the amazing and spectacular Claflin sisters, Tennessee and Victoria," who were described as having been "active—very active—feminists in the 'seventies." These feminists were contrasted with "the modern busybodies of the suffrage and feminist movements," who were "the veriest pigmies in comparison. . . . The miserable, puny outlook of our "radical" feminists of the present day represents a disgraceful degeneration and reflection of the ideals and visions of these two women." The Claflins "possessed spirit, fire, and idealism; whereas the modern champions of feminism strike us in comparison as a loudly clucking, aimless, constipated type of barnyard fowl."

But all of these lexical maneuvers took place while the term "feminism" was still being used in a dizzying variety of ways, some of which had nothing at all to do with women's emancipation, whether radical or tragic, and most of the ideas expressed by radical women found utterance in both feminist and anti-feminist vocabularies. It is probably fair to say that while all these specific vocabularies were chosen in the hope of distinguishing between "vital things" and "trifles," they were not themselves what was vital in the debates and they often owed what force they had to rhetorical maneuvers like Goldman's call for "emancipation from emancipation." For us, at this stage, perhaps nothing is more vital than to recognize our own historical distance from this rather fluid debate, and when we turn back to Goldman's essays it appears that what was most vital to her was *sex*.

———

For Emma Goldman, what was vital was, in fact, *vitality* itself, most often understood as *sex*, but in the most inclusive sense of that term. In an undated manuscript on "The Element of

Sex in Life," she described sex as "the most element force in human life." In her discussion, it becomes hard to distinguish sex from life itself, and her interest in sexual science from a commitment to a sort of sexual *vitalism*. Love and art, procreation and play, and the impetus behind both individual and social development all come back to sex—and not just for human beings.

> To sex we owe more than poetry; we owe the song of birds, all vocal music and the voice itself, the plumage that comes to supreme glory in the bird of paradise, the mane of the lion, the blush of the maiden, the beard of man, and all higher forms of life in plant and animal worlds. It is woven into every fabric of human life and lays its fingers on every custom. To the debit side of the sex account we must charge many silly stupidities and some of the foulest injustices which go to make the thing we call human culture the amazing and variegated mosaic that it is.

Indeed, summing up her position, she claims—in a slight misquotation of Walt Whitman—that "where sex is missing everything is missing."† Sex, in these most abstract moments, is Whitman's "procreant urge of the world," and we might usefully continue the quotation to glimpse the vision that Goldman seems to be affirming:

> Sex contains all, bodies, souls,
> Meanings, proofs, purities, delicacies, results, promulgations,
> Songs, commands, health, pride, the maternal mystery, the seminal milk,
> All hopes, benefactions, bestowals, all the passions, loves, beauties, delights of the earth,

---

† The phrase, from Whitman's poem "A Woman Waits for Me," is "Yet all were lacking if sex were lacking."

> All the governments, judges, gods, follow'd persons of
> the earth,
>> These are contain'd in sex as parts of itself and jus-
>> tifications of itself.

This vision, however, was clearly not one that had been embraced by most of humanity. Instead, various powerful institutions—in the realms of religion, politics, economics and social norms—had attempted to control the element of sex and limit its expression. As a result, Goldman said, "It is not surprising that the most elemental force in human life, sex, should still be degraded and denied." Understood in this way, sex is closely allied with anarchism, which Goldman described as "a living force in the affairs of our life, constantly creating new conditions," sharing as enemies the same group of repressive institutions. In much the same way that Proudhon had connected anarchy with a restless progress, Goldman invites us to link anarchy with sex, and both with life, understood as a transforming force. The influence of Nietzsche is evident in Goldman's approach—even before she calls for a "complete transvaluation of all accepted values"—and her specific critique of feminism echoed familiar Nietzschean themes of decadence, contempt for life and "man," and the opposition of morality to freedom.

Goldman's references to Nietzsche and Whitman—both exuberant writers, excessive in their expressions, and perhaps prone to take things just a little too far—can perhaps serve us when it appears that Goldman has herself been carried away by her passion for life and freedom. There are certainly moments when her generalizations about the character of "woman" in general suggest a different kind of anti-feminism than we would perhaps associate with a woman also praised as a pioneer of anarchist feminism. But a tendency to mix art and preacherly invective, to move unexpectedly from social science to jeremiads—and at times to take it all too far—is certainly not unusual in the literature of anarchism. It is perhaps an occupational hazard for those whose subject matter and values all run towards the unchained and excessive.

Some of Goldman's most vehement expressions were almost certainly intended to provoke scandal, but many of us should also be prepared to be scandalized at odd moments when her work seems to echo views of sex that certainly would not have been controversial to much of her audience. As an "elemental force," but one expressed through very material bodies, sex was, for Goldman, at once innate and socially conditioned, and its conventional expressions manifested some mix of an ideal and the forces committed to its expression. As a result, Goldman was not simply a critic of traditional gender roles. Motherhood, for example, is presented as a natural manifestation of sex, and Goldman shows a continuing interest in the "ideal relation" between "man" and "woman." But this is all consistent with the project of transvaluing values or, as Nietzsche also put it, spiritualizing passions. In the manuscript on "The Element of Sex," Goldman quoted from "Morality as Anti-Naturalness": "All passions have a time when they are fatal only, when, with the weight of their folly, they drag their victim down; and they have a later, very much later period, when they wed with spirit, when they are 'spiritualized.'" It is clear that Goldman was looking towards a time when all passions will be rid of that "weight of folly," and that this conception of the sexual ideal contributed to her defense of sexual passions and practices that might have been considered "unnatural" by many of her contemporaries. It is, however, equally clear that this approach committed her to some defenses of traditional "womanhood," when compared to the "new woman" of her era. The formula of "liberation from liberation" asks us to consider what must be rejected, as well as what must be embraced, in both traditional roles and existing rebellions.

And perhaps nothing more needs to be said, in general, about Emma Goldman's various engagements with "the sex question." If we accept that sex is fundamental, and that it is at once innate and transformative, then we should be prepared to find a similar dynamic in the writings on the subject. If we expect dynamism in the work, then we should be prepared for all the shifts and potential shocks that it contains. Thus prepared, we can apply ourselves to the task of making our way through Goldman's essays.

———

Given the central place of "the element of sex" in Goldman's understanding of life, we might have expected her to produce some more extended treatment of the subject—perhaps a treatise like "The Social Significance of the Modern Drama." There is no question that such a work would have been of interest to many readers, both within and outside of the anarchist movement. What we have, however, is a considerably more fragmented treatment, with the central concern addressed from various directions under a variety of circumstances. We cannot, for the reasons already touched on, simply treat that piecemeal treatment as if it was a unified work, but perhaps we can glimpse the form of that unwritten treatise in the writings available to us.

In fact, taken together, the works at our disposal, if handled with care, provide at least a wonderfully suggestive outline of that treatise. The writings from the 1890s serve as a sort of introduction. "Anarchy and the Sex Question" (1896) and "What Is There in Anarchy for Women?" (1897) place Goldman's concerns regarding "the sex question" explicitly in the context of the agitation for anarchy, even if the these works develop the connection more by juxtaposition than exposition. For example, in the 1897 interview, Goldman spoke of the relation that would replace marriage under conditions of real freedom: "The alliance should be formed, not as it is now, to give the woman a support and home, but because the love is there, and that state of affairs can only be brought about by an internal revolution, in short, Anarchy." It is perhaps not entirely clear which of the previous terms is summarized by "Anarchy," but perhaps the most promising readings simply joins "love," "internal revolution," and "Anarchy" as aspects of the transformation that Goldman anticipated. In these early works, Goldman linked a mass of social ills—poverty, marital unhappiness, prostitution, etc.—to a "system of inequality" hardly distinguishable from "society itself" and manifesting itself equally through Church, State and capitalism. The "anarchist dream" presented in the first poses an alternative system of "perfect equity" as a means of cleansing social relations of these various ills, but by the second the dream had become considerably more ambitious. Talk of an equitable marriage state had been abandoned for a vision of free unions, communal childrearing and the possibility of plural love affairs—all described as part of a vision of "anarchy." Of Goldman's writings, these are among the most compatible with the notion of "women's emancipation," understood as an aspect of the larger anarchist project of human emancipation. But in the short speech "The New Woman" (1898), we find a compact introduction to Goldman's emerging concerns with that movement.

The *Mother Earth* era—and the body of the study—then opens with "The Tragedy of Woman's Emancipation" (1906), in which Goldman introduced the notion of a movement for women's liberation gone so far wrong that women needed to be emancipated from it. Having achieved "merely external emancipation"—and that imperfectly—that movement has ironically only strengthened the grip of the internal tyrannies and "made of the modern woman an artificial being who reminds one of the products of French arboriculture with its arabesque trees and shrubs—pyramids, wheels, and wreaths; anything except the forms which would be reached by the expression of their own inner qualities." In "The White Slave Traffic" (1910), Goldman demonstrated how even the representatives of the most oppressive institutions can claim a part in the struggle for the emancipation of women, provided that evils like prostitution are treated as exceptional, rather than simply one application of a social rule governing all women. No partial solution being possible, the only alternative was a "complete transvaluation of all accepted values," including the "abolition of industrial slavery," widespread public education, and an end to "the Puritanic spirit of the Scarlet Letter days." In the essays "Woman Suffrage" (1914) and "The Woman Suffrage Chameleon" (1917), Goldman demonstrated the extent to which not only had suffrage not advanced the more essential aspects of women's struggles but it had in many cases even intensified the destructive power of authority.

In all those writings, Goldman was unsparing in her scorn for those women who had allowed themselves to be carried along by existing tendencies, but she was not content simply to lay blame. In "The Hypocrisy of Puritanism" (1910), "Jealousy: Causes and a Possible Cure" (ca. 1912), "Victims of Morality" (1913), and the remarkable essay "Marriage and Love" (1914), she explored various aspects of the psychology governing existing relations, along with the possible alternatives.

For those requiring practical applications of these analyses, Goldman provided numerous examples, including the case study "Mary Wollstonecraft" (1911) and the letter concerning the sexuality of Louise Michel (1923), in which the inherent capacities of individual women and the social barriers placed in their paths were depicted vividly. She also recounted her own struggles to disseminate information about birth control, in a pair of articles from 1916. These examinations of the lives of real, talented unite the various aspects of Goldman's analysis, powerfully dramatizing the dilemma in which imperfectly liberated women still find themselves.

Goldman's deportation from the United States in 1919 marks a transition in the study documented here. While she continued to write and speak on similar topics, there is little from the later years that compares to the writings from the *Mother Earth* period. Yet the demands of life in exile did confront Goldman with at least one key opportunity to reconsider her principled position against marriage, and in 1925 she married an acquaintance, James Colton, for the purposes of gaining English citizenship. In 1926, while settled in Canada, and seeking to be admitted again into the United States, she was approached by the Newspaper Enterprise Association to produce a series of articles for U.S. newspapers, dealing with her current views on a variety of questions. Naturally, her newly married status was a topic of curiosity, and the two news stories included here, "Emma's Love Views" and "Feminism's Fight Not Vain," contain Goldman's responses to questions about the potential changes in her views. What they reveal is a personal attempt to apply those views to changed circumstances, which gives another dimension to the more theoretical writings.

Following a general introduction, theoretical exploration and practical application, the undated manuscript "The Element of Sex in Life" can serve us as a kind of summary and review. A close examination of that "most elemental force in human life" seems an ideal way to focus our understanding of Goldman's arguments and take stock of the tools it provides us moving forward. There is certainly no shortage of opportunities for us to go on and apply those tools, whether it is a matter of exploring Goldman's other works or other anarchist writings with a new understanding of what she considered vital, or if it is a question, as it inevitably must be, of using them in the various struggles that face us in our everyday lives. Certainly, whatever we take away from her work, Emma Goldman would have expected us to apply it in the most revolutionary manner possible, to tear down both internal and external tyrannies. She would, I expect, have wanted us to share not just an understanding of what is vital in life, but a vision, like the one she presented in the essay "Love and Marriage," capable of drawing us forward.

> Some day, some day men and women will rise, they will reach the mountain peak, they will meet big and strong and free, ready to receive, to partake, and to bask in the golden rays of love. What fancy, what imagination, what poetic genius can foresee even approximately the potentialities of such a force in the life of men and women. If the world is ever to give birth to true companionship and oneness, not marriage, but love will be the parent.

■ ANARCHY AND THE SEX QUESTION

(1896)

The workingman, whose strength and muscles are so admired by the pale, puny off-springs of the rich, yet whose labour barely brings him enough to keep the wolf of starvation from the door, marries only to have a wife and house-keeper, who must slave from morning till night, who must make every effort to keep down expenses. Her nerves are so tired by the continual effort to make the pitiful wages of her husband support both of them that she grows irritable and no longer is successful in concealing her want of affection for her lord and master, who, alas! soon comes to the conclusion that his hopes and plans have gone astray, and so practically begins to think that marriage is a failure.

The Chain Grows Heavier and Heaver
As the expenses grow larger instead of smaller, the wife, who has lost all of the little strength she had at marriage, likewise feels herself betrayed, and the constant fretting and dread of starvation consumes her beauty in a short time after marriage. She grows despondent, neglects her household duties, and as there are no ties of love and sympathy between herself and her husband to give them strength to face the misery and poverty of their lives, instead of clinging to each other, they become more and more estranged, more and more impatient with each other's faults.

The man cannot, like the millionaire, go to his club, but he goes to a saloon and tries to drown his misery in a glass of beer or whiskey. The unfortunate partner of his misery, who is too honest to seek forgetfulness in the arms of a lover, and who is too poor to allow herself any legitimate recreation or amusement, remains amid the squalid, half-kept surroundings she calls home, and bitterly bemoans the folly that made her a poor man's wife.

Yet there is no way for them to part from each other.

But They Must Wear It

However galling the chain which has been put around their necks by the law and Church may be, it may not be broken unless those two persons decide to permit it to be severed.

Should the law be merciful enough to grant them liberty, every detail of their private life must be dragged to light. The woman is condemned by public opinion and her whole life is ruined. The fear of this disgrace often causes her to break down under the heavy weight of married life without daring to enter a single protest against the outrageous system that has crushed her and so many of her sisters.

The rich endure it to avoid scandal—the poor for the sake of their children and the fear of public opinion. Their lives are one long continuation of hypocrisy and deceit.

The woman who sells her favours is at liberty to leave the man who purchases them at any time, while the respectable wife cannot free herself from a union which is galling to her.

All unnatural unions which are not hallowed by love are prostitution, whether sanctioned by the Church and society or not. Such unions cannot have other than a degrading influence both upon the morals and health of society.

The System Is to Blame

The system which forces women to sell their womanhood and independence to the highest bidder is a branch of the same evil system which gives to a few the right to live on the wealth produced by their fellow-men, 99 percent of whom must toil and slave early and late for barely enough to keep soul and body together, while the fruits of their labour are absorbed by a few idle vampires who are surrounded by every luxury wealth can purchase.

Look for a moment at two pictures of this nineteenth century social system.

Look at the homes of the wealthy, those magnificent palaces whose costly furnishings would put thousands of needy men and women in comfortable circumstances. Look at the dinner parties of these sons and daughters of wealth, a single course of which would feed hundreds of starving ones to whom a full meal of bread washed down by water is a luxury. Look upon these votaries of fashion as they spend their days devising new means of selfish enjoyment—theatres, balls, concerts, yachting, rushing from one part of the globe to another in their mad search for gaiety and pleasure. And then turn a moment and look at those who produce the wealth that pays for these excessive, unnatural enjoyments.

The Other Picture
Look at them herded together in dark, damp cellars, where they never get a breath of fresh air, clothed in rags, carrying their loads of misery from the cradle to the grave, their children running around the streets, naked, starved, without anyone to give them a loving word or tender care, growing up in ignorance and superstition, cursing the day of their birth.

Look at these two startling contrasts, you moralists and philanthropists, and tell me who is to be blamed for it! Those who are driven to prostitution, whether legal or otherwise, or those who drive their victims to such demoralisation?

The cause lies not in prostitution, but in society itself; in the system of inequality of private property and in the State and Church. In the system of legalized theft, murder and violation of the innocent women and helpless children.

The Cure for the Evil
Not until this monster is destroyed will we get rid of the disease which exists in the Senate and all public offices; in the houses of the rich as well as in the miserable barracks of

the poor. Mankind must become conscious of their strength and capabilities, they must be free to commence a new life, a better and nobler life.

Prostitution will never be suppressed by the means employed by the Rev. Dr. Parkhurst and other reformers. It will exist as long as the system exists which breeds it.

When all these reformers unite their efforts with those who are striving to abolish the system which begets crime of every description and erect one which is based upon perfect equity—a system which guarantees every member, man, woman or child, the full fruits of their labour and a perfectly equal right to enjoy the gifts of nature and to attain the highest knowledge—woman will be self-supporting and independent. Her health no longer crushed by endless toil and slavery no longer will she be the victim of man, while man will no longer be possessed of unhealthy, unnatural passions and vices.

An Anarchist's Dream
Each will enter the marriage state with physical strength and moral confidence in each other. Each will love and esteem the other, and will help in working not only for their own welfare, but, being happy themselves, they will desire also the universal happiness of humanity. The offspring of such unions will be strong and healthy in mind and body and will honour and respect their parents, not because it is their duty to do so, but because the parents deserve it. They will be instructed and cared for by the whole community and will be free to follow their own inclinations, and there will be no necessity to teach them sycophancy and the base art of preying upon their fellow-beings. Their aim in life will be, not to obtain power over their brothers, but to win the respect and esteem of every member of the community.

Anarchist Divorce
Should the union of a man and woman prove unsatisfactory and distasteful to them they will in a quiet, friendly manner,

separate and not debase the several relations of marriage by continuing an uncongenial union.

If, instead of persecuting the victims, the reformers of the day will unite their efforts to eradicate the cause, prostitution will no longer disgrace humanity.

To suppress one class and protect another is worse than folly. It is criminal. Do not turn away your heads, you moral man and woman.

Do not allow your prejudice to influence you: look at the question from an unbiased standpoint.

Instead of exerting your strength uselessly, join hands and assist to abolish the corrupt, diseased system.

If married life has not robbed you of honour and self-respect, if you have love for those you call your children, you must, for your own sake as well as theirs, seek emancipation and establish liberty. Then, and not until then, will the evils of matrimony cease.

■ WHAT IS THERE IN ANARCHY FOR WOMEN?

(1897)

"What does anarchy hold out to me—a woman?"

"More to woman than to anyone else—everything which she has not—freedom and equality."

Quickly, earnestly Emma Goldman, the priestess of anarchy, exiled from Russia, feared by police, and now a guest of St. Louis Anarchists,* gave this answer to my question.

I found her at No. 1722 Oregon avenue, an old-style two-story brick house, the home of a sympathizer†—not a relative as has been stated.

I was received by a good-natured, portly German woman, and taken back to a typical German dining-room—everything clean and neat as soap and water could make them. After

---

* EG's eight days in St. Louis, beginning 16 October 1897, were extensively covered by the local press and drew the keen interest of the authorities. When it was erroneously reported that she planned to speak at an open-air meeting on 19 October in front of the city's statue of President Ulysses Grant, Mayor Ziegenheim declared such a gathering illegal and ordered police to bar any attempt. Simultaneously, the city's House of Delegates passed a resolution approving the actions of the mayor and the police department in stifling the "un-American" and "unpatriotic" teachings of a "notorious Anarchist." Under police surveillance, EG spoke the next night at Walhalla Hall to an overflow audience of hundreds. So successful were her meetings in St. Louis that her stay there the following year garnered no coverage at all since, according to *Solidarity*: "the dailies found out they were helping the Anarchists in their propaganda." See *St. Louis Post-Dispatch*, 20 October 1897, *EGP*, reel 47; and *Solidarity*, 1 May 1898, p. 4.

† EG stayed at the home of August Sendlein, an anarchist and cheesemaker

carefully dusting a chair for me with her apron, she took my name back to the bold little free-thinker. I was welcome. I found Emma Goldman sipping her coffee and partaking of bread and jelly, as her morning's repast. She was neatly clad in a percale shirt waist and skirt, with white collar and cuffs, her feet encased in a loose pair of cloth slippers. She doesn't look like a Russian Nihilist who will be sent to Siberia if she ever crosses the frontier of her native land.

"Do you believe in marriage?" I asked.

"I do not," answered the fair little Anarchist, as promptly as before. "I believe that when two people love each other that no judge, minister, or court, or body of people, have anything to do with it. They themselves are the ones to determine the relations which they shall hold with one another. When that relation becomes irksome to either party, or one of the parties, then it can be as quietly terminated as it was formed."

Miss Goldman gave a little nod of her head to emphasize her words, and quite a pretty head it was, crowned with soft brown hair, combed with a bang and brushed to one side. Her eyes are the honest blue, her complexion clear and white. Her nose though rather broad and of a Teutonic type, was well formed. She is short of stature, with a well-rounded figure. Her whole type is more German than Russian. The only serious physical failing that she has is in her eyes. She is so extremely nearsighted that with glasses she can scarcely distinguish print.

"The alliance should be formed," she continued, "not as it is now, to give the woman a support and home, but because the love is there, and that state of affairs can only be brought about by an internal revolution, in short, Anarchy."

She said this as calmly as though she had just expressed an ordinary every-day fact, but the glitter in her eyes showed the "internal revolutions" already at work in her busy brain.

"What does Anarchy promise woman?"

"It holds everything for woman—freedom, equality—everything that woman has not now."

"Isn't woman free?"

"Free! She is the slave of her husband and her children. She should take her part in the business world the same as the man; she should be his equal before the world, as she is in the reality. She is as capable as he, but when she labors she gets less wages. Why? Because she wears skirts instead of trousers."

"But what is to become of the ideal home life, and all that now surrounds the mother, according to a man's idea?"

"Ideal home life, indeed! The woman, instead of being the household queen, told about in story books, is the servant, the mistress, and the slave of both husband and children. She loses her own individuality entirely, even her name she is not allowed to keep. She is the mistress of John Brown or the mistress of Tom Jones; she is that and nothing else. That is the way I think of her."

Miss Goldman has a pleasant accent. She rolls her r's and changes her r's into v's and vice-versa, with a truly Russian pronunciation. She gesticulates a great deal. When she becomes exited her hands and feet and shoulders all help to illustrate her meanings.

"What would you do with the children of the Anarchistic era?"

"The children would be provided with common homes, big boarding schools, where they will be properly cared for and educated and in every way as good, and in most cases, better care than they would receive in their own homes. Very few mothers know how to take proper care of their children, anyway. It is a science only a very few have learned."

"But the women that desire a home life and the care of their own children, the domestic woman, what of her?"

"Oh, of course, the women that desire could keep their children home and confine themselves as strictly as domestic duties as they desired. But it would give those women who desire something broader, a chance to attain any height they desired. With no poor, and no capitalists, and one common purse, this earth will afford the heaven that the Christians are looking for in another world."

She gazed contemplatively in the bottom of the empty coffee cup, as though she saw in imagination the ideal State, already an actuality.

"Who will take care of the children?" I asked, breaking in upon her reverie.

"Every one," she answered, "has tastes and qualifications suiting them to some occupation. I am a trained nurse. I like to care of the sick. So it will be with some women. They will want to care for and teach the children."

"Won't the children lose their love for their parents and feel the lack of their companionship?" A thought of the affectionate little darlings being relegated to a sort of orphan asylum crossed my mind.

"The parents will have the same opportunities of gaining their confidences and affections as they have now. They can spend just as much time there as they please or have them with them just as often as desired. They will be the children of love—healthy, strong-minded—and not as now, in most cases, born of hate and domestic dissensions."

"What do you call love?"

"When a man or a woman finds some quality or qualities in another that they admire and has an overweening desire to please that person, even to the sacrificing of personal feeling; when there is that subtle something drawing them together, that those who love recognize, and feel it in the inmost fiber of their being, then I call that love." She finished speaking and her face was suffused with a rosy blush.

"Can a person love more than one at a time?"

"I don't see why not—if they find the same lovable qualities in several persons. What should prevent one loving the same things in all of them?"

"If we cease to love the man or woman and find some one else, as I said before, we talk it over and quietly change the mode of living. The private affairs of the family need not then be talked over in the courts and become public property. No one can control the affections, therefore there should be no jealousies.

"Heartaches? Oh, yes," she said, sadly, "but not hatred because he or she has tired of the relations. The human race will always have heartaches as long as the heart beats in the breast.

"My religion," she laughingly repeated. "I was of the Hebrew faith when a girl—you know I am a Jewess—but now I am an atheist. No one has been able to prove either the inspiration of the Bible or the existence of a God to my satisfaction. I believe in no hereafter except the hereafter that is found by the physical matter existing in the human body. I think that lives again in some other form, and I don't think that anything once created over is lost—it goes on and on in first one shape, then another. There is no such thing as a soul—it is all the physical matter."

Pretty Miss Goldman finished speaking, and a delicate flush mounted to her cheek as I asked her if she intended to marry.

"No; I don't believe in marriage for others, and I certainly should not preach one thing and practice another."

She sat in an easy attitude with one leg crossed over the other. She is in every sense a womanly looking woman, with masculine mind and courage.

She laughed as she said there were fifty police at her lecture on Wednesday night, and she added, "If there had been a bomb thrown I surely would have been blamed for it."

■ THE NEW WOMAN

**An Address by Emma Goldman before the Liberal
Progressive Society, of Providence, R.I.**

(1898)

The bible story of woman's inequality and inferiority is based
on the declaration of her being created from the rib of man.
Woman cannot without equal opportunity ever rise to equality with him, and hence women are slaves to society as a consequence, and intensified under the marriage code. Despotic
rule causes people to revolt, and they will, do so as a necessity.
Woman is bred to be seen and for outside show, and hence
the sham in society. Her only mission is to marry and to be a
wife and mother, and to cater to a husband who for this will
support her. She thus degrades herself. The present mothers
are not so much to be blamed for this condition, this comes
about by copying their mothers. The mother who is thus
raised cannot have any conception of the true knowledge of
the rearing of the children, i.e., of raising children as a profession, and she never can bring up the child as she ought to
under this system. Mothers are conquered by the child, the
exception being a good mother.

The duty of a wife is considered as an impure subject for
consideration to the young, unmarried woman, and thus the
ignorant girl is forced in the battle unprepared for life consequences. Another great error in the ideal new woman, and
one that is to be condemned, is that of aping the male, seeking
to become masculine, considering that man is superior to
woman. No decent woman can emulate them. We must first
have the New Man. In all things women are the equal of men,

even in the productive field. Even radicals do not differ from the Christians; they do not wish their wives to become radical; even they deem themselves necessary to her protection. So long as she needs protection she is not on equal footing, we need only to protect weaklings. One of the invasive points in the character of man is, that he is too authoritative for the forced progress in woman, and while he has evolved slowly he is making the fatal mistake of securing more liberty for woman through the very thing that was his own enslavement, i.e., authority. Opposition to this will correct this evil.

Contemptible marriage laws and the adherence to them tend to still farther increase the degradation. To assert that freedom of the sex relations is the natural law is interpreted to mean free lust. The law of love governs this as in all matters, love being the fulfillment of the law. Motherhood and its beauty, of which poets have sung and written, is a farce, and cannot be otherwise until we have freedom—economically.

Men are all heroes at home, but cowards abroad. Women, too, would be as unjust at the ballot box as are the men. They are tyrants as well as are the men. Woman, to be free, must be the mutual friend and mate of man. The individual is the ideal liberty. We owe no duty to anyone, save ourselves. When universal woman once comprehends this ideal, then all protective laws, intended for protection, which is indeed her weakness, will disappear, and this adulterous system goes, and with it charity and all its attendant ills. In short, the new woman movement demands an equal advancement by the modern man.

■ THE TRAGEDY OF WOMAN'S EMANCIPATION

(1906)

I begin my article with an admission: Regardless of all political and economic theories, treating of the fundamental differences between the various groups within the human race, regardless of class and race distinctions, regardless of all artificial boundary lines between woman's rights and man's rights, I hold that there is a point where these differentiations may meet and grow into one perfect whole.

With this I do not mean to propose a peace treaty. The general social antagonism which has taken hold of our entire public life to-day, brought about through the force of opposing and contradictory interests, will crumble to pieces when the reorganization of our social life, based upon the principles of economic justice, shall have become a reality.

Peace and harmony between the sexes, and individuals does not necessarily depend on a superficial equalization of human beings; nor does it call for the elimination of individual traits or peculiarities. The problem that confronts us, to-day, and which the nearest future is to solve, is how to be oneself, and yet in oneness with others, to feel deeply with all human beings and still retain one's own innate qualities. This seems to me the basis upon which the mass and the individual, the true democrat and the true individuality, man and woman can meet without antagonism and opposition. The motto should not be forgive one another; it should be, understand one another. The oft-quoted sentence of Mme. de Stael: "To understand everything means to forgive everything," has never particularly appealed to me; it has the odor of the confessional; to forgive one's fellow being conveys the idea of pharisaical superiority. To understand one's being suffices. This admission partly represents the fundamental aspect of my views on the emancipation of woman and its effect upon the entire sex.

Emancipation should make it possible for her to be human in the truest sense. Everything within her that craves assertion and activity should reach expression; and all artificial barriers should be broken and the road towards greater freedom cleared of every trace of centuries of submission and slavery.

This was the original aim of the movement for woman's emancipation. But the results so far achieved have isolated woman and have robbed her of the fountain springs of that happiness which is so essential to her. Merely external emancipation has made of the modern woman an artificial being who reminds one of the products of French arboriculture with its arabesque trees and shrubs—pyramids, wheels and wreaths; anything except the forms which would be reached by the expression of their own inner qualities. Such artificially grown plants of the female sex are to be found in large numbers, especially in the so-called intellectual sphere of our life.

Liberty and equality for woman! What hopes and aspirations these words awakened when they first uttered by some of the noblest and bravest souls of those days. The sun in all its light and glory was to rise upon a new world; in this world woman was to be free to direct her own destiny, an aim certainly worthy of the great enthusiasm, courage, perseverance and ceaseless effort of the tremendous host of pioneer men and women, who staked everything against a world of prejudice and ignorance.

My hopes also move towards that goal, but I insist that the emancipation of woman, as interpreted and practically applied to-day, has failed to reach that great end. Now, woman is confronted with the necessity of emancipation from emancipation, if she really desires to be free. This may sound paradoxical, but is, nevertheless, only too true.

What has she achieved through her emancipation? Equal Suffrage in a few states. Has that purified our political life, as many well-meaning advocates have predicted? Certainly not. Incidentally it is really time that persons with plain, sound judgment should cease to talk about corruption in politics in a boarding-school tone. Corruption of politics has nothing to do with the morals or the laxity of morals of various political personalities. Its cause is altogether a material one. Politics is the reflex of the business and industrial world, the mottoes of which are: "to take is more blessed than to give"; "buy cheap and sell clear"; "one soiled hand washes the other." There is no hope that even woman, with her right to vote, will ever purify politics.

Emancipation has brought woman economic equality with man; that is, she can choose her own profession and trade, but as her past and present physical training have not equipped tier with the necessary strength to compete with man, she is often compelled to exhaust all her energy, use up her vitality and strain every nerve in order to reach the market value. Very few ever succeed, for it is a fact that women doctors, lawyers, architects and engineers are neither met with the same confidence, nor do they receive the same remuneration. And those that do reach that enticing equality generally do so at the expense of their physical and psychical well-being. As to the great mass of working girls and women, how much independence is gained if the narrowness and lack of freedom of the home is exchanged for the narrowness and lack of freedom of the factory, sweat-shop, department store, or office? In addition is the burden which is laid on many women of looking after a "home, sweet home" cold, dreary, disorderly, uninviting—after a day's hard work. Glorious independence! No wonder, that hundreds of girls are so willing to accept the first offer of marriage, sick and tired of their independence behind the counter, or at the sewing or typewriting machine. They are just as ready to marry as girls of middle class people who long to throw off the yoke of parental dependence. A so-called independence which leads only to earning the merest subsistence is not so enticing, not so ideal that one can expect woman to sacrifice everything for it. Our highly praised independence is, after all, but a slow process of dulling and stifling woman's nature, her love instinct and her mother instinct.

Nevertheless, The position of the working girl is far more natural and human than that of her seemingly more fortunate sister in the more cultured professional walk of life. Teachers, physicians, lawyers, engineers, etc., who have to make a dignified, straightened and proper appearance, while the inner life is growing empty and dead.

The narrowness of the existing conception of woman's independence and emancipation; the dread of love for a man who is not her social equal; the fear that love will rob her of her freedom and independence, the horror that love or the joy of motherhood will only hinder her in the full exercise of her profession—all these together make of the emancipated modern woman a compulsory vestal, before whom life, with its great clarifying sorrows and its deep, entrancing joys, rolls on without touching or gripping her soul.

Emancipation as understood by the majority of its adherents and exponents, is of too narrow a scope to permit the boundless joy and ecstasy contained in the deep emotion of the true woman, sweetheart, mother, freedom.

The tragic fate of the self-supporting or economically free woman does not consist of too many, but of too few experiences. True, she surpasses her sister of past generations in knowledge of the world and human nature; and it is because of that that she feels deeply the lack of life's essence, which alone can enrich the human soul and without which the majority of women have become mere automatons.

That such a state of affairs was bound to come was foreseen by those who realized that in the domain of ethics, there still remained decaying ruins of the time of the undisputed superiority of man; ruins that are still considered useful. And, which is more important, a goodly number of the emancipated are unable to get along without them. Every movement that aims at the destruction of existing institutions and the replacement thereof with such as are more advanced more perfect, has followers, who in theory stand for the most extreme radical ideas, and who, nevertheless, in their every-day practice, are like the next best Philistine, feigning respectability and clamoring for the good opinion of their opponents. There are, for example, Socialists, and even Anarchists, who stand for the idea that property is robbery, yet who will grow indignant if anyone owe them the value of a half-dozen pins.

The same Philistine can be found in the movement for woman's emancipation. Yellow journalists and milk and water litterateurs have painted pictures of the emancipated woman that make the hair of the good citizen and his dull companion stand up on end. Every member of the women's rights movement was pictured as a George Sand in her absolute disregard of morality. Nothing was sacred to her. She had no respect for the ideal relation between man and woman. In short, emancipation stood only for a reckless life of lust and sin; regardless of society, religion and morality. The exponents of woman's rights were highly indignant at such a misrepresentation, and, lacking in humor, they exerted all their energy to prove that they were not at all as bad as they were painted, but the very reverse. Of course, as long as woman was the slave of man, she could not be good and pure, but now that she was free and independent she would prove how good she could be and how her influence would have a purifying effect on all institutions in society. True, the movement for woman's rights has broken many old fetters, but it has also established new ones. The great movement of true emancipation has not met with a great race of women, who could look liberty in the face. Their narrow puritanical vision banished man as a disturber and doubtful character out of their emotional life. Man was not to be tolerated at any price, except perhaps as the father of a child, since a child could not very well come to life without a father. Fortunately, the rigid puritanism never will be strong enough to kill the innate craving for motherhood. But woman's freedom is closely allied to man's freedom, and many of my so-called emancipated sisters seem to overlook the fact that a child born in freedom needs the love and devotion of each human being about him, man as well as woman. Unfortunately, it is this narrow conception of human relations that has brought about a great tragedy in the lives of the modern man and woman.

About fifteen years ago appeared a work from the pen of the brilliant Norwegian writer, Laura Marholm, called "Woman, a Character Study." She was one of the first to call attention to the, emptiness and narrowness of the existing conception of woman's emancipation and its tragic effect upon the inner life of woman. In her work she speaks of the fate of several gifted women of international fame: The genius, Eleanora Duse; the great mathematician and writer, Sanja Kovalevskaja; the artist and poet-nature, Marie Bashkirzeff, who died so young. Through each description of the lives of these women of such extraordinary mentality, runs a marked trail of unsatisfied craving for a full, rounded, complete and beautiful life, and the unrest and loneliness resulting from the lack of it. Through these masterly psychological sketches, one cannot help but see that the higher the mental development of woman, the less possible it is for her to meet a congenial mate, who will see in her, not only sex, but also the human being, the friend, comrade and strong individuality who cannot and ought not lose a single trait of her character.

The average man with his self-sufficiency, his ridiculously superior airs of patronage towards the female sex, is an impossibility for woman, as depicted in the "Character Study" by Laura Marholm. Equally impossible for her is the man who can see in her nothing more than her mentality and genius, and who fails to awaken her woman nature.

A rich intellect and a fine soul are usually considered necessary attributes of a deep and beautiful personality. In the case of the modern woman, these attributes serve as a hindrance to the complete assertion of her being. For over one hundred years, the old form of marriage, based on the Bible, "till death us do part" has been denounced as an institution that stands for the sovereignty of the man over the woman, of her of complete submission to his whims and commands and the absolute dependence

upon his name and support. Time and again it has been con-
clusively proven that the old matrimonial relation restricted
woman to the function of man's servant and the bearer of his
children. And yet we find many emancipated women prefer
marriage with all its deficiencies to the narrowness of an unmarried life; narrow and unendurable because of the chains of moral
and social prejudice that cramp and bind her nature.

The cause for such inconsistency on the part of many
advanced women is to be found in the fact that they never
truly understood the meaning of emancipation. They thought
that all that was needed was independence from external
tyrannies; the internal tyrants, far more harmful to life and
growth, such as ethical and social conventions, were left to
take care of themselves; and they have taken care of themselves. They seem to get along beautifully in the heads and
hearts of the most active exponents of woman's emancipation,
as in the heads and hearts of our grandmothers.

These internal tyrants, whether they be in the form of
public opinion or what will mother say, or brother, father, aunt
or relative of any sort; what will Mrs. Grundy, Mr. Comstock,
the employer, the Board of Education say? All these busybodies, moral detectives, jailers of the human spirit, what will
they say? Until woman has learned to defy them all, to stand
firmly on her own ground and to insist upon her own unre-
stricted freedom, to listen to the voice of her nature, whether
it call for life's greatest treasure, love for a man, or her most
glorious privilege, the right to give birth to a child, she cannot
call herself emancipated. How many emancipated women are
brave enough to acknowledge that the voice of love is calling,
wildly beating against, their breasts demanding to be satisfied.

The French novelist, Jean Reibrach, in one of his novels,
"New Beauty," attempts to picture the ideal, beautiful, emancipated woman. This ideal is embodied in a young girl, a physician. She talks very clearly and wisely of how to feed infants,
she is kind and administers medicines free to poor mothers.
She converses with a young man of her acquaintance about the
sanitary conditions of the future and how various bacilli and

germs shall be exterminated by the use of stone walls and floors, and the doing away of rugs and, hangings. She is, of course, very plainly and practically dressed, mostly in black. The young man who, at their first meeting was overawed by the wisdom of his emancipated friend, gradually learns to understand her, and, recognizes one fine day that he loves her. They are young and she is kind and beautiful, and though always in rigid attire, her appearance is softened by her spotlessly clean white collar and cuffs. One would expect that he would tell her of his love, but he is not one to commit romantic absurdities. Poetry and the enthusiasm of love cover their blushing faces before the pure beauty of the lady. He silences the voice of his nature and remains correct. She, too, is always exact, always rational, always well behaved. I fear if they had formed a union, the young man would have risked freezing to death. I must confess that I can see nothing, beautiful in this new beauty, who is as cold as the stone walls and floors she dreams of. Rather would I have the love songs of romantic ages, rather Don Juan, and Madame Venus, rather an elopement by ladder and rope on a moonlight night, followed by a father's curse, mother's moans, and the moral comments of neighbors, than correctness and propriety measured by yardsticks. If love does not know how to give and take without restriction it is not love, but a transaction that never fail to lay stress on a plus and a minus.

The greatest shortcoming of the emancipation of the present day lies in its artificial stiffness and its narrow respectabilities which produce an emptiness in woman's soul that will not let her drink from the fountain of life. I once remarked that there seemed to be a deeper relationship between the old-fashioned mother and hostess, ever on the alert for the happiness of her little ones and the comfort of those she loved and the truly new woman, than between the latter and her average emancipated sister. The disciples of emancipation pure and simple declared me heathen, merely fit for the stake. Their blind zeal did not let them see that my comparison between the old and the new was merely to prove that a goodly number of our grandmothers had more blood in their veins, far more humor and wit, and certainly a greater amount of naturalness, kind-heartedness and simplicity than the majority of our emancipated professional women who fill our colleges, halls of learning, and various offices. This does not mean a wish to return to the past, nor does it condemn woman to her old sphere, the kitchen and the nursery.

Salvation lies in an energetic march onward towards a brighter and clearer future. We are in need of unhampered growth out of old traditions and habits. The movement for woman's emancipation has so far made but the first step in that direction. It is to be hoped that it will gather strength to make another. The right to vote, equal civil rights, are all very good demands, but true emancipation begins neither at the polls nor in courts. It begins in woman's soul. History tells us that every oppressed class gained its true liberation from its masters through its, own efforts. It is necessary that woman learn that lesson, that she realize that her freedom will reach as far as her power to achieve her freedom reaches. It is therefore far more important for her to begin with her inner regeneration to cut loose from the weight of prejudices, traditions, and customs. The demand for various equal rights in every vocation in life is just and fair, but, after all, the most vital right is the right to love and be loved. Indeed if the partial emancipation is to become a complete and true emancipation of woman it will have to do away with the ridiculous notion that to be loved, to be sweetheart and mother, is synonymous with being slave or subordinate. It will have to do away with the absurd notion of the dualism of the sexes, or that man and woman represent two antagonistic worlds.

Pettiness separates, breadth unites. Let us be broad and big. Let us not overlook vital things, because of the bulk of trifles confronting us. A true conception of the relation of the sexes will not admit of conqueror and conquered; it knows of but one great thing: to give one's self boundlessly in order to find oneself richer, deeper, better. That alone can fill the emptiness and replace the tragedy of woman's emancipation with joy, limitless joy.

■ THE WHITE SLAVE TRAFFIC

(1910)

Our reformers have suddenly made a great discovery: the white slave traffic. The papers are full of these "unheard of conditions" in our midst, and the lawmakers are already planning a new set of laws to check the horror.

How is it that an institution, known almost to every child, should have been discovered so suddenly? How is it that this evil, known to all sociologists, should now be made such an important issue?

It is significant that whenever the public mind is to be diverted from a great social wrong, a crusade is inaugurated against indecency, gambling, saloons, etc. And what is the result of such crusades? Gambling is increasing, saloons are doing a lively business through back entrances, prostitution is at its height, and the system of pimps and cadets is but aggravated.

To assume that the recent investigation of the white slave traffic by George Kibbe Turner and others (and by the way, a very superficial investigation), has discovered anything new is, to say the least, very foolish. Prostitution was and is a widespread evil, yet mankind goes on its business, perfectly indifferent to the sufferings and distress of the victims of prostitution. As indifferent, indeed, as mankind has so far remained to our industrial system, or to economic prostitution.

Only when human sorrows are turned into a toy with glaring colors will baby people become interested,—for a while at least. The people are a very fickle baby that must have new toys every day. The "righteous" cry against the white slave traffic is such a toy. It serves to amuse the people for a little while, and it will help to create a few more fat political jobs—parasites who stalk about the world as inspectors, investigators, detectives, etc.

What really is the cause of the trade in women? Not merely white women, but yellow and black women as well. Exploitation, of course: the merciless Moloch of capitalism that fattens on underpaid labor, thus driving thousands of women and girls into prostitution. With Mrs. Warren these girls feel, "Why waste your life working for a few shillings a week in a scullery, eighteen hours a day?"

Naturally, our reformers say nothing about this cause. George Kibbe Turner and all other scribblers know the cause well enough, but it doesn't pay to say anything about it. It is so much more profitable to play the Pharisee, to pretend an outraged morality, than to go to the bottom of things. Yet no less an authority than Dr. Sanger, the author of "The History of Prostitution,"* although not a radical, has this to say:

"A prolific cause of female depravity can be found in the several tables, showing the description of the employment pursued and the wages received by the women previous to their fall, and it will be a question for the political economist to decide how far mere business consideration should be an apology on the part of employers for a reduction in their rates of remuneration, and whether the savings of a small percentage on wages is not more than counterbalanced by the enormous amount of taxation enforced on the public at large to defray the expenses incurred on account of a system of vice, *which is the direct result in many cases of insufficient compensation of honest labor.*"

The economic reason given for prostitution in the above quotation can be found in all works of any consequence dealing with the question. Nor is it necessary to seek

---

* It is a significant fact that Dr. Sanger's book has been excluded from the U.S. mails. Evidently the authorities are not anxious that the public be informed as to the true cause of prostitution.

information in books; one has but to observe everyday life to realize that there are thousands of girls working for two or three dollars a week, withering away in factories and shops, while life passes by in all its joy and glory, leaving them behind. What else are they to do? However, our present-day reformers would do well to look into Dr. Sanger's book. There they will find that out of 2,000 cases under his observation, but few came from the middle classes, from well-ordered conditions, or pleasant homes. By far the largest majority were working girls and working women. Some driven into prostitution through sheer want, others because of a cruel, wretched life at home, others again because of thwarted and crippled physical natures (which I will speak of again later on). Also it will do the maintainers of purity and morality good to learn that out of 2,000 cases 490 were married women, women who lived with their husbands. Evidently there was not much of a guarantee for their safety and purity in the sanctity of marriage.

The very last to cry out against prostitution is our "respectable" class, since it was that class that ushered in prostitution, from Moses to Trinity Church. Dr. H. Bloss, Dr. Alfred Blaschko, Dr. W. W. Sanger, and other eminent writers on this subject convincingly prove that prostitution originated with the so-called upper classes. I quote Dr. Sanger:

"Our most ancient and historical records are believed to be the books of Moses; according to them it must be admitted that prostitutes were common among the Jews, many centuries before Christ. Moses appears to have connived at the intercourse of Jewish young men with foreign prostitutes. He took an Ethiopian woman himself. Assyrian women, Moabites, Midianites, and other neighbors of the Jews established themselves as prostitutes in the land of Israel. Jephtha, the son of a prostitute, became none the less Chief of Israel." Moses evidently believed that therein lay the greatest safeguard for the daughters of his own people. We shall see presently that the Christians were not so considerate of their own daughters, since they did not employ foreigners for that purpose.

The history of the Christian Church will also serve as a history of prostitution, since the two always went hand in hand and furnished thereby great revenues for the Church.

Dr. Sanger cites the case of Pope Clement II., who issued a bull that all prostitutes were to pay a certain amount of their earnings, or that those living on prostitution were compelled to give half their income to the Church. Pope Sixtus IV. received 20,000 ducats from a single brothel, which, incidentally, he himself had built. Nor is it unknown that a great many cloisters and nunneries were in reality nothing else than brothels.

In modern times the Church is a little more careful in that direction. At least, it does not openly demand tribute from prostitutes. It finds it much more profitable to go in for real estate, like Trinity Church, for instance, to rent out death traps at an exorbitant price to those who live off and on prostitution.

Much as I should like to, my space will not admit speaking of prostitution in Egypt, Greece, Rome, and during the Middle Ages. The conditions in the latter period are particularly interesting, inasmuch as prostitution was organized into guilds, presided over by a Brothel Queen. These guilds employed strikes as a medium of improving their condition and keeping a standard price. Certainly that is more practical a method than the one used by the modern wage slave in society.

Never, however, did prostitution reach its present depraved and criminal position, because at no time in past ages was prostitution persecuted and hounded as it is to-day, especially in Anglo-Saxon countries, where Phariseeism is at its height, where each one is busy hiding the skeletons in his own home by pointing to the sore of the other fellow.

But I must not lose sight of the present issue, the white slave traffic. I have already spoken of the economic cause, but I think a cause much deeper and by far of greater importance is the complete ignorance on sex matters. It is a conceded fact that woman has been reared as a sex commodity, and yet she is kept in absolute ignorance of the meaning and importance of sex. Everything dealing with that subject is suppressed, and people who attempt to bring light into this terrible darkness are persecuted and thrown into prison. Yet it is nevertheless true that so long as a girl is not to know how to take care of herself, not to know the function of the most important part of her life, we need not be surprised if she becomes an easy prey to prostitution or any other form of a relationship which degrades her to the position of an object for mere sex gratification.

It is due to this ignorance that the entire life and nature of the girl is thwarted and crippled. We have long ago taken it as a self-evident fact that the boy may follow the call of the wild, that is to say that the boy may, as soon as his sex nature asserts itself, satisfy that nature, but our moralists are scandalized at the very thought that the nature of a girl should assert itself. To the moralist prostitution does not consist so much in the fact that the woman sells her body, but rather that she sells it to many.

Having been looked upon as a mere sex-commodity, the woman's honor, decency, morality, and usefulness have become a part of her sex life. Thus society considers the sex experiences of a man as attributes of his general development, while similar experiences in the life of a woman are looked upon as a terrible calamity, a loss of honor and of all that is good and noble in a human being. This double standard of morality has played no little part in the creation and perpetuation of prostitution. It involves the keeping of the young in absolute ignorance on sex matters, which alleged "innocence," together with an overwrought and stifled sex nature, helps to bring about a state of affairs that our Puritans are so anxious to avoid or prevent. This state of affairs finds a masterly portrayal in Zola's "Fecundity."

Girls, mere children, work in crowded, overheated rooms ten to twelve hours daily at a machine, which tends to keep them in a constant over-excited sex state. Many of these girls haven't any home or comforts of any kind; therefore the street or some place of cheap amusement is the only means of for-getting their daily routine. This naturally brings them into close proximity with the other sex. It is hard to say which of the two factors brings the girl's over-sexed condition to a climax, but it certainly is the most natural thing that a climax should follow. That is the first step toward prostitution. Nor is the girl to be held responsible for it. On the contrary, it is alto-gether the fault of society, the fault of our lack of understand-ing, of lack of appreciation of life in the making; especially is it the criminal fault of our moralists, who condemn a girl for all eternity because she has gone from "the path of virtue"; that is, because her first sex experience has taken place without the sanction of the Church or State.

The girl finds herself a complete outcast, with the doors of home and society closed in her face. Her entire training and tradition are such that the girl herself feels depraved and fallen, and therefore has no ground to stand upon, or any hold that will lift her up, instead of throwing her down. Thus society creates the victims that it afterwards vainly attempts to get rid of.

Much stress is laid on white slaves being imported into America. How would America ever retain her virtue if she didn't have Europe to help her out? I will not deny that this may be the case in some instances, any more than I will deny that there are emissaries of Germany and other countries luring economic slaves into America, but I absolutely deny that prostitution is recruited, to any appreciable extent, from Europe. It may be true that the majority of prostitutes of New York City are foreigners, but that is only because the majority of the population is foreign. The moment we go to any other American city, to Chicago or the middle West, we shall find that the number of foreign prostitutes is by far a minority.

Equally exaggerated is the belief that the majority of street girls in this city were engaged in this business before they came to America. Most of the girls speak excellent English, they are Americanized in habits and appearance,—a thing absolutely impossible unless they have lived in this country many years. That is, they were driven into prostitution by American conditions, by the thoroughly American custom for excessive display of finery and clothes, which, of course, necessitates money, money that can not be earned in shops or factories. The equanimity of the moralists is not disturbed by the respectable woman gratifying her clothesophobia by marrying for money; why are they so outraged if the poor girl sells herself for the same reason? The only difference lies in the amount received, and of course in the seal society either gives or withholds.

I am sure that no one will accuse me of nationalist tendencies. I am glad to say that I have developed out of that, as out of many other prejudices. If, therefore, I resent the statement that Jewish prostitutes are imported, it is not because of any Judaistic sympathies, but because of the fact inherent in the lives of these people. No one but the most superficial will claim that the Jewish girls migrate to strange lands unless they have some tie or relation that brings them there. The Jewish girl is not adventurous. Until recent years, she had never left home, not even so far as the next village or town, unless it were to visit some relative. Is it then credible that Jewish girls would leave their parents or families, travel thousands of miles to strange lands, through the influence and promises of strange forces? Go to any of the large incoming steamers and see for yourself if these girls do not come either with their parents, brothers, aunts, or other kinsfolk. There may be exceptions, of course, but to state that a large number of Jewish girls are imported for prostitution, or any other purpose, is simply not to know the Jewish psychology.

On the other hand, it speaks of very little business ability on the part of importers of the white slaves, if they assume that the girls from the peasant regions of Poland, Bohemia, or Hungary in their native peasant crude state and attire would make a profitable business investment. These poor ignorant girls, in their undeveloped state, with their shawls about their heads, look much too unattractive to even the most stupid man. It therefore follows that before they can be made fit for business, they, too, must be Americanized, which would require not merely a week or a month, but considerable time. They must at least learn the rudiments of English, but more than anything else they must learn American shrewdness, in order to protect themselves against the many uniformed cadets, who prey on them and fleece them at every step.

To ascribe the increase of prostitution to alleged importation, to the growth of the cadet system, or similar causes, is highly superficial. I have already referred to the former. As to the cadet system, abhorrent as it is, we must not ignore the fact that it is essentially a phase of modern prostitution,—a phase accentuated by suppression and graft, resulting from sporadic crusades against the social evil.

The origin of the cadets, as an institution, can be traced to the Lexow investigation in New York City, in 1894. Thanks to that moral spasm, keepers of brothels, as well as unfortunate victims of the street, were turned over to the tender mercies of the police. The inevitable consequence of exorbitant bribes and the penitentiary followed.

While comparatively protected in the brothels, where they represented a certain value, the unfortunate girls now found themselves on the street, absolutely at the mercy of the graft-greedy police. Desperate, needing protection and longing for affection, these girls naturally proved an easy prey to cadets, themselves the result of the spirit of our commercial age. Thus the cadet system was the direct outgrowth of police persecution, graft, and attempted suppression of prostitution. It were sheer folly to confute this modern phase of the social evil with the causes of the latter.

The serious student of this problem realizes that legislative enactments, stringent laws, and similar methods can not possibly eradicate, nor even ameliorate this evil. Those best familiar with the subject agree on this vital point. Dr. Alfred Blaschko, an eminent authority, convincingly proves in his *Prostitution im 19. Jahrhundert* that governmental suppression and moral crusades accomplish nothing save driving the evil into secret channels, multiplying its dangers to the community. In this claim he is supported by such thorough students as Havelock Ellis, Dr. H. Bloss, and others.

Mere suppression and barbaric enactment can serve but to embitter and further degrade the unfortunate victims of ignorance and stupidity. The latter has reached its highest expression in the proposed law to make humane treatment of prostitutes a crime, punishing anyone sheltering a prostitute with five years imprisonment and $10,000 fine. Such an attitude merely exposes the terrible lack of understanding of the true causes of prostitution, as a social factor, as well as manifesting the Puritanic spirit of the Scarlet Letter days.

An educated public opinion, freed from the legal and moral hounding of the prostitute, can alone help to ameliorate present conditions. Wilful shutting of eyes and ignoring of the evil, as an actual social factor of modern life, can but aggravate matters. We must rise above our foolish notions of "better than thou," and learn to recognize in the prostitute a product of social conditions. Such a realization will sweep away the attitude of hypocrisy and insure a greater understanding and more humane treatment. As to a thorough eradication of prostitution, nothing can accomplish that save a complete transvaluation of all accepted values—especially the moral ones—coupled with the abolition of industrial slavery.

■ WOMAN SUFFRAGE

(1910)

We boast of the age of advancement, of science, and progress. Is it not strange, then, that we still believe in fetich worship? True, our fetiches have different form and substance, yet in their power over the human mind they are still as disastrous as were those of old.

Our modern fetich is universal suffrage. Those who have not yet achieved that goal fight bloody revolutions to obtain it, and those who have enjoyed its reign bring heavy sacrifice to the altar of this omnipotent deity. Woe to the heretic who dare question that divinity!

Woman, even more than man, is a fetich worshipper, and though her idols may change, she is ever on her knees, ever holding up her hands, ever blind to the fact that her god has feet of clay. Thus woman has been the greatest supporter of all deities from time immemorial. Thus, too, she has had to pay the price that only gods can exact,—her freedom, her heart's blood, her very life.

Nietzsche's memorable maxim, "When you go to woman, take the whip along," is considered very brutal, yet Nietzsche expressed in one sentence the attitude of woman towards her gods.

Religion, especially the Christian religion, has condemned woman to the life of an inferior, a slave. It has thwarted her nature and fettered her soul, yet the Christian religion has no greater supporter, none more devout, than woman. Indeed, it is safe to say that religion would have long ceased to be a factor in the lives of the people, if it were not for the support it receives from woman. The most ardent church-workers, the most tireless missionaries the world over, are women, always sacrificing on the altar of the gods that have chained her spirit and enslaved her body.

The insatiable monster, war, robs woman of all that is dear and precious to her. It exacts her brothers, lovers, sons, and in return gives her a life of loneliness and despair. Yet the greatest supporter and worshiper of war is woman. She it is who instills the love of conquest and power into her children; she it is who whispers the glories of war into the ears of her little ones, and who rocks her baby to sleep with the tunes of trumpets and the noise of guns. It is woman, too, who crowns the victor on his return from the battlefield. Yes, it is woman who pays the highest price to that insatiable monster, war.

Then there is the home. What a terrible fetich it is! How it saps the very life-energy of woman,—this modern prison with golden bars. Its shining aspect blinds woman to the price she would have to pay as wife, mother, and housekeeper. Yet woman clings tenaciously to the home, to the power that holds her in bondage.

It may be said that because woman recognizes the awful toll she is made to pay to the Church, State, and the home, she wants suffrage to set herself free. That may be true of the few; the majority of suffragists repudiate utterly such blasphemy. On the contrary, they insist always that it is woman suffrage which will make her a better Christian and home keeper, a staunch citizen of the State. Thus suffrage is only a means of strengthening the omnipotence of the very Gods that woman has served from time immemorial.

What wonder, then, that she should be just as devout, just as zealous, just as prostrate before the new idol, woman suffrage. As of old, she endures persecution, imprisonment, torture, and all forms of condemnation, with a smile on her face. As of old, the most enlightened, even, hope for a miracle from the twentieth-century deity,—suffrage. Life, happiness, joy, freedom, independence,—all that, and more, is to spring from suffrage. In her blind devotion woman does not see what people of intellect perceived fifty years ago: that suffrage is an evil, that it has only helped to enslave people, that it has but closed their eyes that they may not see how craftily they were made to submit.

Woman's demand for equal suffrage is based largely on the contention that woman must have the equal right in all affairs of society. No one could, possibly, refute that, if suffrage were a right. Alas, for the ignorance of the human mind, which can see a right in an imposition. Or is it not the most brutal imposition for one set of people to make laws that another set is coerced by force to obey? Yet woman clamors for that "golden opportunity" that has wrought so much misery in the world, and robbed man of his integrity and self-reliance; an imposition which has thoroughly corrupted the people, and made them absolute prey in the hands of unscrupulous politicians.

The poor, stupid, free American citizen! Free to starve, free to tramp the highways of this great country, he enjoys universal suffrage, and, by that right, he has forged chains about his limbs. The reward that he receives is stringent labor laws prohibiting the right of boycott, of picketing, in fact, of everything, except the right to be robbed of the fruits of his labor. Yet all these disastrous results of the twentieth-century fetich have taught woman nothing. But, then, woman will purify politics, we are assured.

Needless to say, I am not opposed to woman suffrage on the conventional ground that she is not equal to it. I see neither physical, psychological, nor mental reasons why woman should not have the equal right to vote with man. But that can not possibly blind me to the absurd notion that woman will accomplish that wherein man has failed. If she would not make things worse, she certainly could not make them better. To assume, therefore, that she would succeed in purifying something which is not susceptible of purification, is to credit her with supernatural powers. Since woman's greatest misfortune has been that she was looked upon as either angel or devil, her true salvation lies in being placed on earth; namely, in being considered human, and therefore subject to all human follies and mistakes. Are we, then, to believe that two errors will make a right? Are we to assume that the poison already inherent in politics will be decreased, if women were to enter the political arena? The most ardent suffragists would hardly maintain such a folly.

As a matter of fact, the most advanced students of universal suffrage have come to realize that all existing systems of political power are absurd, and are completely inadequate to meet the pressing issues of life. This view is also borne out by a statement of one who is herself an ardent believer in woman suffrage, Dr. Helen L. Sumner. In her able work on *Equal Suffrage*, she says: "In Colorado, we find that equal suffrage serves to show in the most striking way the essential rottenness and degrading character of the existing system." Of course, Dr. Sumner has in mind a particular system of voting, but the same applies with equal force to the entire machinery of the representative system. With such a basis, it is difficult to understand how woman, as a political factor, would benefit either herself or the rest of mankind.

But, say our suffrage devotees, look at the countries and States where female suffrage exists. See what woman has accomplished—in Australia, New Zealand, Finland, the Scandinavian countries, and in our own four States, Idaho, Colorado, Wyoming, and Utah. Distance lends enchantment—or, to quote a Polish formula—"it is well where we are not." Thus one would assume that those countries and States are unlike other countries or States, that they have greater freedom, greater social and economic equality, a finer appreciation of human life, deeper understanding of the great social struggle, with all the vital questions it involves for the human race.

The women of Australia and New Zealand can vote, and help make the laws. Are the labor conditions better there than they are in England, where the suffragettes are making such a heroic struggle? Does there exist a greater motherhood, happier and freer children than in England? Is woman there no longer considered a mere sex commodity? Has she emancipated herself from the Puritanical double standard of morality for men and women? Certainly none but the ordinary female stump politician will dare answer these questions in the affirmative. If that be so, it seems ridiculous to point to Australia and New Zealand as the Mecca of equal suffrage accomplishments.

On the other hand, it is a fact to those who know the real political conditions in Australia, that politics have gagged labor by enacting the most stringent labor laws, making strikes without the sanction of an arbitration committee a crime equal to treason.

Not for a moment do I mean to imply that woman suffrage is responsible for this state of affairs. I do mean, however, that there is no reason to point to Australia as a wonder-worker of woman's accomplishment, since her influence has been unable to free labor from the thralldom of political bossism.

Finland has given woman equal suffrage; nay, even the right to sit in Parliament. Has that helped to develop a greater heroism, an intenser zeal than that of the women of Russia? Finland, like Russia, smarts under the terrible whip of the bloody Tsar. Where are the Finnish Perovskaias, Spiridonovas, Figners, Breshkovskaias? Where are the countless numbers of Finnish young girls who cheerfully go to Siberia for their cause? Finland is sadly in need of heroic liberators. Why has the ballot not created them? The only Finnish avenger of his people was a man, not a woman, and he used a more effective weapon than the ballot.

As to our own States where women vote, and which are constantly being pointed out as examples of marvels, what has been accomplished there through the ballot that women do not to a large extent enjoy in other States; or that they could not achieve through energetic efforts without the ballot?

True, in the suffrage States women are guaranteed equal rights to property; but of what avail is that right to the mass of women without property, the thousands of wage workers, who live from hand to mouth? That equal suffrage did not, and cannot, affect their condition is admitted even by Dr. Sumner, who certainly is in a position to know. As an ardent suffragist, and having been sent to Colorado by the Collegiate Equal Suffrage League of New York State to collect material in favor of suffrage, she would be the last to say anything derogatory; yet we are informed that "equal suffrage has but slightly affected the economic conditions of women. That women do not receive equal pay for equal work, and that, though woman in Colorado has enjoyed school suffrage since 1876, women teachers are paid less than in California." On the other hand, Miss Sumner fails to account for the fact that although women have had school suffrage for thirty-four years, and equal suffrage since 1894, the census in Denver alone a few months ago disclosed the fact of fifteen thousand defective school children. And that, too, with mostly women in the educational department, and also notwithstanding that women in Colorado have passed the "most stringent laws for child and animal protection." The women of Colorado "have taken great interest in the State institutions for the care of dependent, defective, and delinquent children." What a horrible indictment against woman's care and interest, if one city has fifteen thousand defective children. What about the glory of woman suffrage, since it has failed utterly in the most important social issue, the child? And where is the superior sense of justice that woman was to bring into the political field? Where was it in 1903, when the mine owners waged a guerilla war against the Western Miners' Union; when General Bell established a reign of terror, pulling men out of bed at night, kidnapping them across the border line, throwing them into bull pens, declaring "to hell with the Constitution, the club is the Constitution"? Where were the women politicians then, and why did they not exercise the power of their vote? But they did. They helped to defeat the most fair-minded and liberal man, Governor Waite. The latter had to make way for the tool of the mine kings, Governor Peabody, the enemy of labor, the Tsar of Colorado. "Certainly male suffrage could have done nothing worse." Granted. Wherein, then, are the advantages to woman and society from woman suffrage? The oft-repeated assertion that woman will purify politics is also but a myth. It is not borne out by the people who know the political conditions of Idaho, Colorado, Wyoming, and Utah.

Woman, essentially a purist, is naturally bigoted and relentless in her effort to make others as good as she thinks they ought to be. Thus, in Idaho, she has disfranchised her sister of the street, and declared all women of "lewd character" unfit to vote. "Lewd" not being interpreted, of course, as prostitution *in* marriage. It goes without saying that illegal prostitution and gambling have been prohibited. In this regard the law must needs be of feminine gender: it always prohibits. Therein all laws are wonderful. They go no further, but their very tendencies open all the floodgates of hell. Prostitution and gambling have never done a more flourishing business than since the law has been set against them.

In Colorado, the Puritanism of woman has expressed itself in a more drastic form. "Men of notoriously unclean lives, and men connected with saloons, have been dropped from politics since women have the vote."* Could Brother Comstock do more? Could all the Puritan fathers have done more? I wonder how many women realize the gravity of this would-be feat. I wonder if they understand that it is the very thing which, instead of elevating woman, has made her a political spy, a contemptible pry into the private affairs of people, not so much for the good of the cause, but because, as a Colorado woman said, "they like to get into houses they have never been in, and find out all they can, politically and otherwise."† Yes, and into the human soul and its minutest nooks and corners. For nothing satisfies the craving of most women so much as scandal. And when did she ever enjoy such opportunities as are hers, the politician's?

"Notoriously unclean lives, and men connected with the saloons." Certainly, the lady vote gatherers can not be

---

* *Equal Suffrage*. Dr. Helen Sumner.
† *Equal Suffrage.*

accused of much sense of proportion. Granting even that these busybodies can decide whose lives are clean enough for that eminently clean atmosphere, politics, must it follow that saloon-keepers belong to the same category? Unless it be American hypocrisy and bigotry, so manifest in the principle of Prohibition, which sanctions the spread of drunkenness among men and women of the rich class, yet keeps vigilant watch on the only place left to the poor man. If no other reason, woman's narrow and purist attitude toward life makes her a greater danger to liberty wherever she has political power. Man has long overcome the superstitions that still engulf woman. In the economic competitive field, man has been compelled to exercise efficiency, judgment, ability, competency. He therefore had neither time nor inclination to measure everyone's morality with a Puritanic yardstick. In his political activities, too, he has not gone about blindfolded. He knows that quantity and not quality is the material for the political grinding mill, and, unless he is a sentimental reformer or an old fossil, he knows that politics can never be anything but a swamp.

Women who are at all conversant with the process of politics, know the nature of the beast, but in their self-sufficiency and egotism they make themselves believe that they have but to pet the beast, and he will become as gentle as a lamb, sweet and pure. As if women have not sold their votes, as if women politicians cannot be bought! If her body can be bought in return for material consideration, why not her vote? That it is being done in Colorado and in other States, is not denied even by those in favor of woman suffrage.

As I have said before, woman's narrow view of human affairs is not the only argument against her as a politician superior to man. There are others. Her life-long economic parasitism has utterly blurred her conception of the meaning of equality. She clamors for equal rights with man, yet we learn that "few women care to canvas in undesirable districts."[‡]

‡ Dr. Helen L. Sumner.

How little equality means to them compared with the Russian women, who face hell itself for their ideal!

Woman demands the same rights as man, yet she is indignant that her presence does not strike him dead: he smokes, keeps his hat on, and does not jump from his seat like a flunkey. These may be trivial things, but they are nevertheless the key to the nature of American suffragists. To be sure, their English sisters have outgrown these silly notions. They have shown themselves equal to the greatest demands on their character and power of endurance. All honor to the heroism and sturdiness of the English suffragettes. Thanks to their energetic, aggressive methods, they have proved an inspiration to some of our own lifeless and spineless ladies. But after all, the suffragettes, too, are still lacking in appreciation of real equality. Else how is one to account for the tremendous, truly gigantic effort set in motion by those valiant fighters for a wretched little bill which will benefit a handful of propertied ladies, with absolutely no provision for the vast mass of working women? True, as politicians they must be opportunists, must take half-measures if they can not get all. But as intelligent and liberal women they ought to realize that if the ballot is a weapon, the disinherited need it more than the economically superior class, and that the latter already enjoy too much power by virtue of their economic superiority.

The brilliant leader of the English suffragettes, Mrs. Emmeline Pankhurst, herself admitted, when on her American lecture tour, that there can be no equality between political superiors and inferiors. If so, how will the workingwomen of England, already inferior economically to the ladies who are benefited by the Shackleton bill,§ be able to work with their political superiors, should the bill pass? Is it not probable that the class of Annie Keeney, so full of zeal, devotion,

§ Mr. Shackleton was a labor leader. It is therefore self-evident that he should introduce a bill excluding his own constituents. The English Parliament is full of such Judases.

and martyrdom, will be compelled to carry on their backs their female political bosses, even as they are carrying their economic masters. They would still have to do it, were universal suffrage for men and women established in England. No matter what the workers do, they are made to pay, always. Still, those who believe in the power of the vote show little sense of justice when they concern themselves not at all with those whom, as they claim, it might serve most.

The American suffrage movement has been, until very recently, altogether a parlor affair, absolutely detached from the economic needs of the people. Thus Susan B. Anthony, no doubt an exceptional type of woman, was not only indifferent but antagonistic to labor; nor did she hesitate to manifest her antagonism when, in 1869, she advised women to take the places of striking printers in New York.⁵ I do not know whether her attitude had changed before her death.

There are, of course, some suffragists who are affiliated with workingwomen—the Women's Trade Union League, for instance; but they are a small minority, and their activities are essentially economic. The rest look upon toil as a just provision of Providence. What would become of the rich, if not for the poor? What would become of these idle, parasitic ladies, who squander more in a week than their victims earn in a year, if not for the eighty million wage-workers? Equality, who ever heard of such a thing?

Few countries have produced such arrogance and snobbishness as America. Particularly is this true of the American woman of the middle class. She not only considers herself the equal of man, but his superior, especially in her purity, goodness, and morality. Small wonder that the American suffragist claims for her vote the most miraculous powers. In her exalted conceit she does not see how truly enslaved she is, not so much by man, as by her own silly notions and traditions. Suffrage can not ameliorate that sad fact; it can only accentuate it, as indeed it does.

¶ *Equal Suffrage.*

One of the great American women leaders claims that woman is entitled not only to equal pay, but that she ought to be legally entitled even to the pay of her husband. Failing to support her, he should be put in convict stripes, and his earnings in prison be collected by his equal wife. Does not another brilliant exponent of the cause claim for woman that her vote will abolish the social evil, which has been fought in vain by the collective efforts of the most illustrious minds the world over? It is indeed to be regretted that the alleged creator of the universe has already presented us with his wonderful scheme of things, else woman suffrage would surely enable woman to outdo him completely.

Nothing is so dangerous as the dissection of a fetich. If we have outlived the time when such heresy was punishable by the stake, we have not outlived the narrow spirit of condemnation of those who dare differ with accepted notions. Therefore I shall probably be put down as an opponent of woman. But that can not deter me from looking the question squarely in the face. I repeat what I have said in the beginning: I do not believe that woman will make politics worse; nor can I believe that she could make it better. If, then, she cannot improve on man's mistakes, why perpetrate the latter?

History may be a compilation of lies; nevertheless, it contains a few truths, and they are the only guide we have for the future. The history of the political activities of men proves that they have given him absolutely nothing that he could not have achieved in a more direct, less costly, and more lasting manner. As a matter of fact, every inch of ground he has gained has been through a constant fight, a ceaseless struggle for self-assertion, and not through suffrage. There is no reason whatever to assume that woman, in her climb to emancipation, has been, or will be, helped by the ballot.

In the darkest of all countries, Russia, with her absolute despotism, woman has become man's equal, not through the ballot, but by her will to be and to do. Not only has she conquered for herself every avenue of learning and vocation, but she has won man's esteem, his respect, his comradeship;

aye, even more than that: she has gained the admiration, the respect of the whole world. That, too, not through suffrage, but by her wonderful heroism, her fortitude, her ability, will-power, and her endurance in her struggle for liberty. Where are the women in any suffrage country or State that can lay claim to such a victory? When we consider the accomplishments of woman in America, we find also that something deeper and more powerful than suffrage has helped her in the march to emancipation.

It is just sixty-two years ago since a handful of women at the Seneca Falls Convention set forth a few demands for their right to equal education with men, and access to the various professions, trades, etc. What wonderful accomplishments, what wonderful triumphs! Who but the most ignorant dare speak of woman as a mere domestic drudge? Who dare suggest that this or that profession should not be open to her? For over sixty years she has molded a new atmosphere and a new life for herself. She has become a world-power in every domain of human thought and activity. And all that without suffrage, without the right to make laws, without the "privilege" of becoming a judge, a jailer, or an executioner.

Yes, I may be considered an enemy of woman; but if I can help her see the light, I shall not complain.

The misfortune of woman is not that she is unable to do the work of a man, but that she is wasting her life-force to outdo him, with a tradition of centuries which has left her physically incapable of keeping pace with him. Oh, I know some have succeeded, but at what cost, at what terrific cost! The import is not the kind of work woman does, but rather the quality of the work she furnishes. She can give suffrage or the ballot no new quality, nor can she receive anything from it that will enhance her own quality. Her development, her freedom, her independence, must come from and through herself. First, by asserting herself as a personality, and not as a sex commodity. Second, by refusing the right to anyone over her body; by refusing to bear children, unless she wants them; by refusing to be a servant to God, the State, society, the husband, the family, etc., by making her life simpler, but deeper and richer. That is, by trying to learn the meaning and substance of life in all its complexities, by freeing herself from the fear of public opinion and public condemnation. Only that, and not the ballot, will set woman free, will make her a force hitherto unknown in the world, a force for real love, for peace, for harmony; a force of divine fire, of life-giving; a creator of free men and women.

■ MARRIAGE AND LOVE

(1910)

The popular notion about marriage and love is that they are synonymous, that they spring from the same motives, and cover the same human needs. Like most popular notions this also rests not on actual facts, but on superstition.

Marriage and love have nothing in common; they are as far apart as the poles; are, in fact, antagonistic to each other. No doubt some marriages have been the result of love. Not, however, because love could assert itself only in marriage; much rather is it because few people can completely outgrow a convention. There are to-day large numbers of men and women to whom marriage is naught but a farce, but who submit to it for the sake of public opinion. At any rate, while it is true that some marriages are based on love, and while it is equally true that in some cases love continues in married life, I maintain that it does so regardless of marriage, and not because of it.

On the other hand, it is utterly false that love results from marriage. On rare occasions one does hear of a miraculous case of a married couple falling in love after marriage, but on close examination it will be found that it is a mere adjustment to the inevitable. Certainly the growing-used to each other is far away from the spontaneity, the intensity, and beauty of love, without which the intimacy of marriage must prove degrading to both the woman and the man.

Marriage is primarily an economic arrangement, an insurance pact. It differs from the ordinary life insurance agreement only in that it is more binding, more exacting. Its returns are insignificantly small compared with the investments. In taking out an insurance policy one pays for it in dollars and cents, always at liberty to discontinue payments. If, however, woman's premium is a husband, she pays for it with her name, her privacy, her self-respect, her very life, "until death doth part." Moreover, the marriage insurance condemns her to life-long dependency, to parasitism, to complete uselessness, individual as well as social. Man, too, pays his toll, but as his sphere is wider, marriage does not limit him as much as woman. He feels his chains more in an economic sense.

Thus Dante's motto over Inferno applies with equal force to marriage: "Ye who enter here leave all hope behind."

That marriage is a failure none but the very stupid will deny. One has but to glance over the statistics of divorce to realize how bitter a failure marriage really is. Nor will the stereotyped Philistine argument that the laxity of divorce laws and the growing looseness of woman account for the fact that: first, every twelfth marriage ends in divorce; second, that since 1870 divorces have increased from 28 to 73 for every hundred thousand population; third, that adultery, since 1867, as ground for divorce, has increased 270.8 per cent.; fourth, that desertion increased 369.8 per cent.

Added to these startling figures is a vast amount of material, dramatic and literary, further elucidating this subject. Robert Herrick, in *Together*; Pinero, in *Mid-Channel*; Eugene Walter, in *Paid in Full*, and scores of other writers are discussing the barrenness, the monotony, the sordidness, the inadequacy of marriage as a factor for harmony and understanding.

The thoughtful social student will not content himself with the popular superficial excuse for this phenomenon. He will have to dig down deeper into the very life of the sexes to know why marriage proves so disastrous.

Edward Carpenter says that behind every marriage stands the life-long environment of the two sexes; an environment so different from each other that man and woman must remain strangers. Separated by an insurmountable wall of superstition, custom, and habit, marriage has not the potentiality of developing knowledge of, and respect for, each other, without which every union is doomed to failure.

Henrik Ibsen, the hater of all social shams, was probably the first to realize this great truth. Nora leaves her husband, not—as the stupid critic would have it—because she is tired of her responsibilities or feels the need of woman's rights, but because she has come to know that for eight years she had lived with a stranger and borne him children. Can there be any thing more humiliating, more degrading than a life long proximity between two strangers? No need for the woman to know anything of the man, save his income. As to the knowledge of the woman—what is there to know except that she has a pleasing appearance? We have not yet outgrown the theologic myth that woman has no soul, that she is a mere appendix to man, made out of his rib just for the convenience of the gentleman who was so strong that he was afraid of his own shadow.

Perchance the poor quality of the material whence woman comes is responsible for her inferiority. At any rate, woman has no soul—what is there to know about her? Besides, the less soul a woman has the greater her asset as a wife, the more readily will she absorb herself in her husband. It is this slavish acquiescence to man's superiority that has kept the marriage institution seemingly intact for so long a period. Now that woman is coming into her own, now that she is actually growing aware of herself as a being outside of the master's grace, the sacred institution of marriage is gradually being undermined, and no amount of sentimental lamentation can stay it.

From infancy, almost, the average girl is told that marriage is her ultimate goal; therefore her training and education must be directed towards that end. Like the mute beast fattened for slaughter, she is prepared for that. Yet, strange to say, she is allowed to know much less about her function as wife and mother than the ordinary artisan of his trade. It is indecent and filthy for a respectable girl to know anything of the marital relation. Oh, for the inconsistency of respectability, that needs the marriage vow to turn something which is filthy into the purest and most sacred arrangement that none dare question or criticize. Yet that is exactly the attitude of the average upholder of marriage. The prospective wife and mother is kept in complete ignorance of her only asset in the competitive field—sex. Thus she enters into life-long relations with a man only to find herself shocked, repelled, outraged beyond measure by the most natural and healthy instinct, sex. It is safe to say that a large percentage of the unhappiness, misery, distress, and physical suffering of matrimony is due to the criminal ignorance in sex matters that is being extolled as a great virtue. Nor is it at all an exaggeration when I say that more than one home has been broken up because of this deplorable fact.

If, however, woman is free and big enough to learn the mystery of sex without the sanction of State or Church, she will stand condemned as utterly unfit to become the wife of a "good" man, his goodness consisting of an empty head and plenty of money. Can there be anything more outrageous than the idea that a healthy, grown woman, full of life and passion, must deny nature's demand, must subdue her most intense craving, undermine her health and break her spirit, must stunt her vision, abstain from the depth and glory of sex experience until a "good" man comes along to take her unto himself as a wife? That is precisely what marriage means. How can such an arrangement end except in failure? This is one, though not the least important, factor of marriage, which differentiates it from love.

Ours is a practical age. The time when Romeo and Juliet risked the wrath of their fathers for love, when Gretchen exposed herself to the gossip of her neighbors for love, is no more. If, on rare occasions, young people allow themselves the luxury of romance, they are taken in care by the elders, drilled and pounded until they become "sensible."

The moral lesson instilled in the girl is not whether the man has aroused her love, but rather is it, "How much?" The important and only God of practical American life: Can the man make a living? Can he support a wife? That is the only thing that justifies marriage. Gradually this saturates every thought of the girl; her dreams are not of moonlight and kisses, of laughter and tears; she dreams of shopping tours and bargain counters. This soul-poverty and sordidness are the elements inherent in the marriage institution. The State and the Church approve of no other ideal, simply because it is the one that necessitates the State and Church control of men and women.

Doubtless there are people who continue to consider love above dollars and cents. Particularly is this true of that class whom economic necessity has forced to become self-supporting. The tremendous change in woman's position, wrought by that mighty factor, is indeed phenomenal when we reflect that it is but a short time since she has entered the industrial arena. Six million women wage-earners; six million women, who have the equal right with men to be exploited, to be robbed, to go on strike; aye, to starve even. Anything more, my lord? Yes, six million wage-workers in every walk of life, from the highest brain work to the most difficult menial labor in the mines and on the railroad tracks; yes, even detectives and policemen. Surely the emancipation is complete.

Yet with all that, but a very small number of the vast army of women wage-workers look upon work as a permanent issue, in the same light as does man. No matter how decrepit the latter, he has been taught to be independent, self-supporting. Oh, I know that no one is really independent in our economic tread mill; still, the poorest specimen of a man hates to be a parasite; to be known as such, at any rate.

The woman considers her position as worker transitory, to be thrown aside for the first bidder. That is why it is infinitely harder to organize women than men. "Why should I join a union? I am going to get married, to have a home." Has she not been taught from infancy to look upon that as her ultimate calling? She learns soon enough that the home, though not so large a prison as the factory, has more solid doors and bars. It has a keeper so faithful that naught can escape him.

The most tragic part, however, is that the home no longer frees her from wage slavery; it only increases her task.

According to the latest statistics submitted before a Committee "on labor and wages, and congestion of Population," ten per cent of the wage workers in New York City alone are married, yet they must continue to work at the most poorly paid labor in the world. Add to this horrible aspect the drudgery of house work, and what remains of the protection and glory of the home? As a matter of fact, even the middle class girl in marriage can not speak of her home, since it is the man who creates her sphere. It is not important whether the husband is a brute or a darling. What I wish to prove is that marriage guarantees woman a home only by the grace of her husband. There she moves about in *his* home, year after year until her aspect of life and human affairs becomes as flat, narrow, and drab as her surroundings. Small wonder if she becomes a nag, petty, quarrelsome, gossipy, unbearable, thus driving the man from the house. She could not go, if she wanted to; there is no place to go. Besides, a short period of married life, of complete surrender of all faculties, absolutely incapacitates the average woman for the outside world. She becomes reckless in appearance, clumsy in her movements, dependent in her decisions, cowardly in her judgment, a weight and a bore, which most men grow to hate and despise. Wonderfully inspiring atmosphere for the bearing of life, is it not?

But the child, how is it to be protected, if not for marriage? After all, is not that the most important consideration? The sham, the hypocrisy of it! Marriage protecting the child, yet thousands of children destitute and homeless. Marriage protecting the child, yet orphan asylums and reformatories overcrowded, the Society for the Prevention of Cruelty to Children keeping busy in rescuing the little victims from "loving" parents, to place them under more loving care, the Gerry Society. Oh, the mockery of it!

Marriage may have the power to "bring the horse to water," but has it ever made him drink? The law will place the father under arrest, and put him in convict's clothes; but has that ever stilled the hunger of the child? If the parent has no work, or if he hides his identity, what does marriage do then? It invokes the law to bring the man to "justice," to put him safely behind closed doors; his labor, however, goes not to the child, but to the State. The child receives but a blighted memory of its father's stripes.

As to the protection of the woman,—therein lies the curse of marriage. Not that it really protects her, but the very idea is so revolting, such an outrage and insult on life, so degrading to human dignity, as to forever condemn this parasitic institution.

It is like that other paternal arrangement—capitalism. It robs man of his birthright, stunts his growth, poisons his body, keeps him in ignorance, in poverty and dependence, and then institutes charities that thrive on the last vestige of man's self-respect.

The institution of marriage makes a parasite of woman, an absolute dependent. It incapacitates her for life's struggle, annihilates her social consciousness, paralyzes her imagination, and then imposes its gracious protection, which is in reality a snare, a travesty on human character.

If motherhood is the highest fulfillment of woman's nature, what other protection does it need save love and freedom? Marriage but defiles, outrages, and corrupts her fulfillment. Does it not say to woman, Only when you follow me shall you bring forth life? Does it not condemn her to the block, does it not degrade and shame her if she refuses to buy her right to motherhood by selling herself? Does not marriage only sanction motherhood, even though conceived in hatred, in compulsion? Yet, if motherhood be of free choice, of love, of ecstasy, of defiant passion, does it not place a crown of thorns upon an innocent head and carve in letters of blood the hideous epithet, Bastard? Were marriage to contain all the virtues claimed for it, its crimes against motherhood would exclude it forever from the realm of love.

Love, the strongest and deepest element in all life, the harbinger of hope, of joy, of ecstasy; love, the defier of all laws, of all conventions; love, the freest, the most powerful moulder of human destiny; how can such an all-compelling force be synonymous with that poor little State and Church-begotten weed, marriage?

Free love? As if love is anything but free! Man has bought brains, but all the millions in the world have failed to buy love. Man has subdued bodies, but all the power on earth has been unable to subdue love. Man has conquered whole nations, but all his armies could not conquer love. Man has chained and fettered the spirit, but he has been utterly help-less before love. High on a throne, with all the splendor and pomp his gold can command, man is yet poor and desolate, if love passes him by. And if it stays, the poorest hovel is radiant with warmth, with life and color. Thus love has the magic power to make of a beggar a king. Yes, love is free; it can dwell in no other atmosphere. In freedom it gives itself unreservedly, abundantly, completely. All the laws on the statutes, all the courts in the universe, cannot tear it from the soil, once love has taken root. If, however, the soil is sterile, how can mar-riage make it bear fruit? It is like the last desperate struggle of fleeting life against death.

Love needs no protection; it is its own protection. So long as love begets life no child is deserted, or hungry, or famished for the want of affection. I know this to be true. I know women who became mothers in freedom by the men they loved. Few children in wedlock enjoy the care, the protection, the devotion free motherhood is capable of bestowing.

The defenders of authority dread the advent of a free motherhood, lest it will rob them of their prey. Who would fight wars? Who would create wealth? Who would make the policeman, the jailer, if woman were to refuse the indis-criminate breeding of children? The race, the race! shouts the king, the president, the capitalist, the priest. The race must be preserved, though woman be degraded to a mere machine,—and the marriage institution is our only safety valve against the pernicious sex-awakening of woman. But in vain these frantic efforts to maintain a state of bondage. In vain, too, the edicts of the Church, the mad attacks of rulers, in vain even the arm of the law. Woman no longer wants to be a party to the production of a race of sickly, feeble, decrepit, wretched human beings, who have neither the strength nor moral courage to throw off the yoke of poverty and slavery. Instead she desires fewer and better children, begotten and reared in love and through free choice; not by compulsion, as marriage imposes. Our pseudo-moralists have yet to learn the deep sense of responsibility toward the child, that love in freedom has awakened in the breast of woman. Rather would she forego forever the glory of motherhood than bring forth life in an atmosphere that breathes only destruction and death. And if she does become a mother, it is to give to the child the deepest and best her being can yield. To grow with the child is her motto; she knows that in that manner alone can she help build true manhood and womanhood.

Ibsen must have had a vision of a free mother, when, with a master stroke, he portrayed Mrs. Alving. She was the ideal mother because she had outgrown marriage and all its horrors, because she had broken her chains, and set her spirit free to soar until it returned a personality, regenerated and strong. Alas, it was too late to rescue her life's joy, her Oswald; but not too late to realize that love in freedom is the only condition of a beautiful life. Those who, like Mrs. Alving, have paid with blood and tears for their spiritual awakening, repudiate marriage as an imposition, a shallow, empty mockery. They know, whether love last but one brief span of time or for eternity, it is the only creative, inspiring, elevating basis for a new race, a new world.

In our present pygmy state love is indeed a stranger to most people. Misunderstood and shunned, it rarely takes root; or if it does, it soon withers and dies. Its delicate fiber can not endure the stress and strain of the daily grind. Its soul is too complex to adjust itself to the slimy woof of our social fabric. It weeps and moans and suffers with those who have need of it, yet lack the capacity to rise to love's summit.

Some day, some day men and women will rise, they will reach the mountain peak, they will meet big and strong and free, ready to receive, to partake, and to bask in the golden rays of love. What fancy, what imagination, what poetic genius can foresee even approximately the potentialities of such a force in the life of men and women. If the world is ever to give birth to true companionship and oneness, not marriage, but love will be the parent.

■ THE HYPOCRISY OF PURITANISM

(1910)

Speaking of Puritanism in relation to American art, Mr. Gutzon Borglum said:

"Puritanism has made us self-centered and hypocritical for so long, that sincerity and reverence for what is natural in our impulses have been fairly bred out of us, with the result that there can be neither truth nor individuality in our art."

Mr. Borglum might have added that Puritanism has made life itself impossible. More than art, more than estheticism, life represents beauty in a thousand variations; it is, indeed, a gigantic panorama of eternal change. Puritanism, on the other hand, rests on a fixed and immovable conception of life; it is based on the Calvinistic idea that life is a curse, imposed upon man by the wrath of God. In order to redeem himself man must do constant penance, must repudiate every natural and healthy impulse, and turn his back on joy and beauty.

Puritanism celebrated its reign of terror in England during the sixteenth and seventeenth centuries, destroying and crushing every manifestation of art and culture. It was the spirit of Puritanism which robbed Shelley of his children, because he would not bow to the dicta of religion. It was the same narrow spirit which alienated Byron from his native land, because that great genius rebelled against the monotony, dullness, and pettiness of his country. It was Puritanism, too, that forced some of England's freest women into the conventional lie of marriage: Mary Wollstonecraft and, later, George Eliot. And recently Puritanism has demanded another toll—the life of Oscar Wilde. In fact, Puritanism has never ceased to be the most pernicious factor in the domain of John Bull, acting as censor of the artistic expression of his people, and stamping its approval only on the dullness of middle-class respectability.

It is therefore sheer British jingoism which points to America as the country of Puritanic provincialism. It is quite true that our life is stunted by Puritanism, and that the latter is killing what is natural and healthy in our impulses. But it is equally true that it is to England that we are indebted for transplanting this spirit on American soil. It was bequeathed to us by the Pilgrim fathers. Fleeing from persecution and oppression, the Pilgrims of Mayflower fame established in the New World a reign of Puritanic tyranny and crime. The history of New England, and especially of Massachusetts, is full of the horrors that have turned life into gloom, joy and despair, naturalness into disease, honesty and truth into hideous lies and hypocrisies. The ducking-stool and whipping-post, as well as numerous other devices of torture, were the favorite English methods for American purification.

Boston, the city of culture, has gone down in the annals of Puritanism as the "Bloody Town." It rivaled Salem, even, in her cruel persecution of unauthorized religious opinions. On the now famous Common a half-naked woman, with a baby in her arms, was publicly whipped for the crime of free speech; and on the same spot Mary Dyer, another Quaker woman, was hanged in 1659. In fact, Boston has been the scene of more than one wanton crime committed by Puritanism. Salem, in the summer of 1692, killed eighteen people for witchcraft. Nor was Massachusetts alone in driving out the devil by fire and brimstone. As Canning justly said: "The Pilgrim fathers infested the New World to redress the balance of the Old." The horrors of that period have found their most supreme expression in the American classic, *The Scarlet Letter*.

Puritanism no longer employs the thumbscrew and lash; but it still has a most pernicious hold on the minds and feelings of the American people. Naught else can explain the power of a Comstock. Like the Torquemadas of ante-bellum days, Anthony Comstock is the autocrat of American morals; he dictates the standards of good and evil, of purity and vice. Like a thief in the night he sneaks into the private lives of the people, into their most intimate relations. The system of espionage established by this man Comstock puts to shame the infamous Third Division of the Russian secret police. Why does the public tolerate such an outrage on its liberties? Simply because Comstock is but the loud expression of the Puritanism bred in the Anglo-Saxon blood, and from whose thralldom even liberals have not succeeded in fully emancipating themselves. The visionless and leaden elements of the old Young Men's and Women's Christian Temperance Unions, Purity Leagues, American Sabbath Unions, and the Prohibition Party, with Anthony Comstock as their patron saint, are the grave diggers of American art and culture.

Europe can at least boast of a bold art and literature which delve deeply into the social and sexual problems of our time, exercising a severe critique of all our shams.

As with a surgeon's knife every Puritanic carcass is dissected, and the way thus cleared for man's liberation from the dead weights of the past. But with Puritanism as the constant check upon American life, neither truth nor sincerity is possible. Nothing but gloom and mediocrity to dictate human conduct, curtail natural expression, and stifle our best impulses. Puritanism in this the twentieth century is as much the enemy of freedom and beauty as it was when it landed on Plymouth Rock. It repudiates; but being absolutely ignorant as to the real functions of human emotions, Puritanism is itself the creator of the most unspeakable vices.

The entire history of asceticism proves this to be only too true. The Church, as well as Puritanism, has fought the flesh as something evil; it had to be subdued and hidden at all cost. The result of this vicious attitude is only now beginning to be recognized by modern thinkers and educators. They realize that "nakedness has a hygienic value as well as a spiritual significance, far beyond its influences in allaying the natural inquisitiveness of the young or acting as a preventative of morbid emotion. It is an inspiration to adults who have long outgrown any youthful curiosities. The vision of the essential and eternal human form, the nearest thing to us in all the world, with its vigor and its beauty and its grace, is one of the prime tonics of life." But the spirit of purism has so perverted the human mind that it has lost the power to appreciate the beauty of nudity, forcing us to hide the natural form under the plea of chastity. Yet chastity itself is but an artificial imposition upon nature, expressive of a false shame of the human form. The modern idea of chastity, especially in reference to woman, its greatest victim, is but the sensuous exaggeration of our natural impulses. "Chastity varies with the amount of clothing," and hence Christians and purists forever hasten to cover the "heathen" with tatters, and thus convert him to goodness and chastity.

Puritanism, with its perversion of the significance and functions of the human body, especially in regard to woman, has condemned her to celibacy, or to the indiscriminate breeding of a diseased race, or to prostitution. The enormity of this crime against humanity is apparent when we consider the results. Absolute sexual continence is imposed upon the unmarried woman, under pain of being considered immoral or fallen, with the result of producing neurasthenia, impotence, depression, and a great variety of nervous complaints involving diminished power of work, limited enjoyment of life, sleeplessness, and preoccupation with sexual desires and imaginings. The arbitrary and pernicious dictum of total continence probably also explains the mental inequality of the sexes. Thus Freud believes that the intellectual inferiority of so many women is due to the inhibition of thought imposed upon them for the purpose of sexual repression. Having thus suppressed the natural sex desires of the unmarried woman, Puritanism, on the other hand, blesses her married sister for incontinent fruitfulness in wedlock. Indeed, not merely blesses her, but forces the woman, oversexed by previous repression, to bear children, irrespective of weakened physical condition or economic inability to rear a large family.

Prevention, even by scientifically determined safe methods, is absolutely prohibited; nay, the very mention of the subject is considered criminal.

Thanks to this Puritanic tyranny, the majority of women soon find themselves at the ebb of their physical resources. Ill and worn, they are utterly unable to give their children even elementary care. That, added to economic pressure, forces many women to risk utmost danger rather than continue to bring forth life. The custom of procuring abortions has reached such vast proportions in America as to be almost beyond belief. According to recent investigations along this line, seventeen abortions are committed in every hundred pregnancies. This fearful percentage represents only cases which come to the knowledge of physicians. Considering the secrecy in which this practice is necessarily shrouded, and the consequent professional inefficiency and neglect, Puritanism continuously exacts thousands of victims to its own stupidity and hypocrisy.

Prostitution, although hounded, imprisoned, and chained, is nevertheless the greatest triumph of Puritanism. It is its most cherished child, all hypocritical sanctimoniousness notwithstanding. The prostitute is the fury of our century, sweeping across the "civilized" countries like a hurricane, and leaving a trail of disease and disaster. The only remedy Puritanism offers for this ill-begotten child is greater repression and more merciless persecution. The latest outrage is represented by the Page Law, which imposes upon the State of New York the terrible failure and crime of Europe, namely, registration and identification of the unfortunate victims of Puritanism. In equally stupid manner purism seeks to check the terrible scourge of its own creation—venereal diseases. Most disheartening it is that this spirit of obtuse narrow-mindedness has poisoned even our so-called liberals, and has blinded them into joining the crusade against the very things born of the hypocrisy of Puritanism—prostitution and its results. In willful blindness Puritanism refuses to see that the true method of prevention is the one which makes it clear to all that "venereal diseases are not a mysterious or terrible thing, the penalty of the sin of the flesh, a sort of shameful evil branded by purist malediction, but an ordinary disease which may be treated and cured." By its methods of obscurity, disguise, and concealment, Puritanism has furnished favorable conditions for the growth and spread of these diseases. Its bigotry is again most strikingly demonstrated by the senseless attitude in regard to the great discovery of Prof. Ehrlich, hypocrisy veiling the important cure for syphilis with vague allusions to a remedy for "a certain poison."

The almost limitless capacity of Puritanism for evil is due to its entrenchment behind the State and the law. Pretending to safeguard the people against "immorality," it has impregnated the machinery of government and added to its usurpation of moral guardianship the legal censorship of our views, feelings, and even of our conduct.

Art, literature, the drama, the privacy of the mails, in fact, our most intimate tastes, are at the mercy of this inexorable tyrant. Anthony Comstock, or some other equally ignorant policeman, has been given power to desecrate genius, to soil and mutilate the sublimest creation of nature—the human form. Books dealing with the most vital issues of our lives, and seeking to shed light upon dangerously obscured problems, are legally treated as criminal offenses, and their helpless authors thrown into prison or driven to destruction and death.

Not even in the domain of the Tsar is personal liberty daily outraged to the extent it is in America, the stronghold of the Puritanic eunuchs. Here the only day of recreation left to the masses, Sunday, has been made hideous and utterly impossible. All writers on primitive customs and ancient civilization agree that the Sabbath was a day of festivities, free from care and duties, a day of general rejoicing and merrymaking. In every European country this tradition continues to bring some relief from the humdrum and stupidity of our Christian era. Everywhere concert halls, theaters, museums, and gardens are filled with men, women, and children, particularly workers with their families, full of life and joy, forgetful of the ordinary rules and conventions of their every-day existence. It is on that day that the masses demonstrate what life might really mean in a sane society, with work stripped of its profit-making, soul-destroying purpose.

Puritanism has robbed the people even of that one day. Naturally, only the workers are affected: our millionaires have their luxurious homes and elaborate clubs. The poor, however, are condemned to the monotony and dullness of the American Sunday. The sociability and fun of European outdoor life is here exchanged for the gloom of the church, the stuffy, germ-saturated country parlor, or the brutalizing atmosphere of the back-room saloon. In Prohibition States the people lack even the latter, unless they can invest their meager earnings in quantities of adulterated liquor. As to Prohibition, every one knows what a farce it really is. Like all other achievements of Puritanism it, too, has but driven the "devil" deeper into the human system. Nowhere else does one meet so many drunkards as in our Prohibition towns. But so long as one can use scented candy to abate the foul breath of hypocrisy, Puritanism is triumphant. Ostensibly Prohibition is opposed to liquor for reasons of health and economy, but the very spirit of Prohibition being itself abnormal, it succeeds but in creating an abnormal life.

Every stimulus which quickens the imagination and raises the spirits, is as necessary to our life as air. It invigorates the body, and deepens our vision of human fellowship. Without stimuli, in one form or another, creative work is impossible, nor indeed the spirit of kindliness and generosity. The fact that some great geniuses have seen their reflection in the goblet too frequently, does not justify Puritanism in attempting to fetter the whole gamut of human emotions. A Byron and a Poe have stirred humanity deeper than all the Puritans can ever hope to do. The former have given to life meaning and color; the latter are turning red blood into water, beauty into ugliness, variety into uniformity and decay. Puritanism, in whatever expression, is a poisonous germ. On the surface everything may look strong and vigorous; yet the poison works its way persistently, until the entire fabric is doomed. With Hippolyte Taine, every truly free spirit has come to realize that "Puritanism is the death of culture, philosophy, humor, and good fellowship; its characteristics are dullness, monotony, and gloom."

■ MARY WOLLSTONECRAFT, HER TRAGIC LIFE AND HER PASSIONATE STRUGGLE FOR FREEDOM

(1911)

The Pioneers of human progress are like the Seagulls, they behold new coasts, new spheres of daring thought, when their co-voyagers see only the endless stretch of water. They send joyous greetings to the distant lands. Intense, yearning, burning faith pierces the clouds of doubt, because the sharp ears of the harbingers of life discern from the maddening roar of the waves, the new message, the new symbol for humanity.

The latter does not grasp the new, dull, and inert, it meets the pioneer of truth with misgivings and resentment, as the disturber of its peace, as the annihilator of all stable habits and traditions.

Thus the pathfinders are heard only by the few, because they will not tread the beaten tracks, and the mass lacks the strength to follow into the unknown.

In conflict with every institution of their time since they will not compromise, it is inevitable that the advance guards should become aliens to the very ones they wish to serve; that they should be isolated, shunned, and repudiated by the nearest and dearest of kin. Yet the tragedy every pioneer must experience is not the lack of understanding—it arises from the fact that having seen new possibilities for human advancement, the pioneers can not take root in the old, and with the new still far off they become outcast roamers of the earth, restless seekers for the things they will never find.

They are consumed by the fires of compassion and sympathy for all suffering and with all their fellows, yet they are compelled to stand apart from their surroundings. Nor need they ever hope to receive the love their great souls crave, for such is the penalty of a great spirit, that what he receives is but nothing compared to what he gives.

Such was the fate and tragedy of Mary Wollstonecraft. What she gave the World, to those she loved, towered high above the average possibility to receive, nor could her burning, yearning soul content itself with the miserly crumbs that fall from the barren table of the average life.

Mary Wollstonecraft came into the World at a time when her sex was in chattel slavery: owned by the father while at home and passed on as a commodity to her husband when married. It was indeed a strange World that Mary entered into on the twenty-seventh of April 1759, yet not very much stranger than our own. For while the human race has no doubt progressed since that memorable moment, Mary Wollstonecraft is still very much the pioneer, far ahead of our own time.

She was one of many children of a middle-class family, the head of which lived up to his rights as master by tyrannizing his wife and children and squandering his capital in idle living and feasting. Who could stay him, the creator of the universe? As in many other things, so have his rights changed little, since Mary's father's time. The family soon found itself in dire want, but how were middle-class girls to earn their own living with every avenue closed to them? They had but one calling, that was marriage. Mary's sister probably realized that. She married a man she did not love in order to escape the misery of the parents' home. But Mary was made of different material, a material so finely woven it could not fit into coarse surroundings. Her intellect saw the degradation of her sex, and her soul—always at white heat against every wrong—rebelled against the slavery of half of the human race. She determined to stand on her own feet. In that determination she was strengthened by her friendship with Fannie Blood, who herself had made the first step towards emancipation by working for her own support. But even without Fannie Blood as a great spiritual force in Mary's life, nor yet even without the economic factor, she was destined by her very nature to become the Iconoclast of the false Gods whose standards the World demanded her to obey. Mary was a born rebel, one who would have created rather than submit to any form set up for her.

It has been said that nature uses a vast amount of human material to create one genius. The same holds good of the true rebel, the true pioneer. Mary was born and not made through this or that individual incident in her surroundings. The treasure of her soul, the wisdom of her life's philosophy, the depth of her World of thought, the intensity of her battle for human emancipation and especially her indomitable struggle for the liberation of her own sex, are even today so far ahead of the average grasp that we may indeed claim for her the rare exception which nature has created but once in a century. Like the Falcon who soared through space in order to behold the Sun and then paid for it with his life, Mary drained the cup of tragedy, for such is the price of wisdom.

Much has been written and said about this wonderful champion of the eighteenth century, but the subject is too vast and still very far from being exhausted. The woman's movement of today and especially the suffrage movement will find in the life and struggle of Mary Wollstonecraft much that would show them the inadequacy of mere external gain as a means of freeing their sex. No doubt much has been accomplished since Mary thundered against women's economic and political enslavement, but has that made her free? Has it added to the depth of her being? Has it brought joy and cheer in her life? Mary's own tragic life proves that economic and social rights for women alone are not enough to fill her life, nor yet enough to fill any deep life, man or woman. It is not true that the deep and fine man—I do not mean the mere male—differs very largely from the deep and fine woman. He too seeks for beauty and love, for harmony and understanding. Mary realized that, because she did not limit herself to her own sex, she demanded freedom for the whole human race.

To make herself economically independent, Mary first taught school and then accepted a position as Governess to the pampered children of a pampered lady, but she soon realized that she was unfit to be a servant and that she must turn to something that would enable her to live, yet at the same time would not drag her down. She learned the bitterness and humiliation of the economic struggle. It was not so much the lack of external comforts, that galled Mary's soul, but it was the lack of inner freedom which results from poverty and dependence which made her cry out, "*How can anyone profess to be a friend to freedom yet not see that poverty is the greatest evil.*"

Fortunately for Mary and posterity, there existed a rare specimen of humanity, which we of the twentieth century still lack, the daring and liberal Publisher Johnson. He was the first to publish the works of Blake, of Thomas Paine, of Godwin and of all the rebels of his time without any regard to material gain. He also saw Mary's great possibilities and engaged her as proofreader, translator, and contributor to his paper, the *Analytical Review*. He did more. He became her most devoted friend and advisor. In fact, no other man in Mary's life was so staunch and understood her difficult nature, as did that rare man. Nor did she ever open up her soul as unreservedly to any one as she did to him. Thus she writes in one of her analytical moments:

"*Life is but a jest. I am a strange compound of weakness and resolution. There is certainly a great defect in my mind—my wayward heart creates its own misery. Why I am made this I cannot tell; and, till I can form some idea of the whole of my existence, I must be content to weep and dance like a child, long for a toy and be tired of it as soon as I get it. We must each of us wear a fool's cap, but mine alas has lost its bells and is grown so heavy, I find it intolerably troublesome.*"

That Mary should write thus of herself to Johnson shows that there must have been a beautiful comradeship between them. At any rate, thanks to her friend she found relief from the terrible struggle. She found also intellectual food. Johnson's rooms were the rendezvous of the intellectual elite of London. Thomas Paine, Godwin, Dr. Fordyce, the Painter Fuseli, and many others gathered there to discuss all the great subjects of their time.

Mary came into their sphere and became the very center of that intellectual bustle. Godwin relates how he came to hear Tom Paine at an evening arranged for him, but instead he had to listen to Mary Wollstonecraft, her conversational powers like everything else about her inevitably stood in the center of the stage.

Thus Mary could soar through space, her spirit reaching out to great heights. The opportunity soon offered itself. The erstwhile champion of English liberalism, the great Edmund Burke, delivered himself of a sentimental sermon against the French Revolution. He had met the fair Marie Antoinette and bewailed her lot at the hands of the infuriated people of Paris. His middle-class sentimentality saw in the greatest of all uprisings only the surface and not the terrible wrongs the French people endured before they were driven to their acts. But Mary Wollstonecraft saw and her reply to the mighty Burke, *The Vindication of the Rights of Man*, is one of the most powerful pleas for the oppressed and disinherited ever made.

It was written at white heat, for Mary had followed the revolution intently. Her force, her enthusiasm, and, above all, her logic and clarity of vision proved this erstwhile schoolmistress to be possessed of a tremendous brain and of a deep and passionately throbbing heart. That such should emanate from a woman was like a bomb explosion, unheard of before. It shocked the World at large, but gained for Mary the respect and affection of her male contemporaries. They felt no doubt, that she was not only their equal, but in many respects, superior to most of them.

"When you call yourself a friend of liberty, ask your own heart whether it would not be more consistent to style yourself the champion of Property, the adorer of the golden image which power has set up?

"Security of Property! behold in a few words the definition of English liberty. But softly, it is only the property of the rich that is secure, the man who lives by the sweat of his brow has no asylum from oppression."

Think of the wonderful penetration in a woman more than one hundred years ago. Even today there are few among our so-called reformers, certainly very few among the women reformers, who see as clearly as this giant of the eighteenth Century. She understood only too well that mere political changes are not enough and do not strike deep into the evils of Society.

Mary Wollstonecraft on Passion:

"The regulating of passion is not always wise. On the contrary, it should seem that one reason why men have a superior judgment and more fortitude than women is undoubtedly this, that they give a freer scope to the grand passion and by more frequently going astray enlarge their minds.

"Drunkenness is due to lack of better amusement rather than to innate viciousness, crime is often the outcome of a superabundant life.

"The same energy which renders a man a daring villain would have rendered him useful to society had that society been well organized."

Mary was not only an intellectual, she was, as she says herself, possessed of a wayward heart. That is she craved love and affection. It was therefore but natural for her to be carried away by the beauty and passion of the Painter Fuseli, but whether he did not reciprocate her love, or because he lacked courage at the critical moment, Mary was forced to go through her first experience of love and pain. She certainly was not the kind of a woman to throw herself on any man's neck. Fuseli was an easy-go-lucky sort and easily carried away by Mary's beauty. But he had a wife, and the pressure of public opinion was too much for him. Be it as it may, Mary suffered keenly and fled to France to escape the charms of the artist.

Biographers are the last to understand their subject or else they would not have made so much ado of the Fuseli episode, for it was nothing else. Had the loud-mouthed Fuseli been as free as Mary to gratify their sex attraction, Mary would probably have settled down to her normal life. But he lacked courage and Mary, having been sexually starved, could not easily quench the aroused senses.

However, it required but a strong intellectual interest to bring her back to herself. And that interest she found in the stirring events of the French Revolution.

However, it was before the Fuseli incident that Mary added to her *Vindication of the Rights of Man* the *Vindication of the Rights of Woman*, a plea for the emancipation of her sex. It is not that she held man responsible for the enslavement of woman. Mary was too big and too universal to place the blame on one sex. She emphasized the fact that woman herself is a hindrance to human progress because she persists in being a sex object rather than a personality, a creative force in life. Naturally, she maintained that man has been the tyrant so long that he resents any encroachment upon his domain, but she pleaded that it was as much for his as for woman's sake that she demanded economic, political, and sexual freedom for women as the only solution to the problem of human emancipation.

"The laws respecting women made an absurd unit of a man and his wife and then by the easy transition of only considering him as responsible, she is reduced to a mere cypher."

Nature has certainly been very lavish when she fashioned Mary Wollstonecraft. Not only has she endowed her with a tremendous brain, but she gave her great beauty and charm. She also gave her a deep soul, deep both in joy and sorrow. Mary was therefore doomed to become the prey of more than one infatuation. Her love for Fuseli soon made way for a more terrible, more intense love, the greatest force in her life, one that tossed her about as a willess, helpless toy in the hands of fate.

Life without love for a character like Mary is inconceivable, and it was her search and yearning for love which hurled her against the rock of inconsistency and despair.

While in Paris, Mary met in the house of Thomas Paine where she had been welcomed as a friend, the vivacious, handsome, and elemental American, [Gilbert] Imlay. If not for Mary's love for him the world might never have known of this Gentleman. Not that he was ordinary, Mary could not have loved him with that mad passion which nearly wrecked her life. He had distinguished himself in the American War and had written a thing or two, but on the whole he would never have set the World on fire. But he set Mary on fire and held her in a trance for a considerable time.

The very force of her infatuation for him excluded harmony, but is it a matter of blame as far as Imlay is concerned? He gave her all he could, but her insatiable hunger for love could never be content with little, hence the tragedy. Then too, he was a roamer, an adventurer, an explorer into the territory of female hearts. He was possessed by the Wanderlust, could not rest at peace long anywhere. Mary needed peace, she also needed what she had never had in her family, the quiet and warmth of a home. But more than anything else she needed love, unreserved, passionate love. Imlay could give her nothing and the struggle began shortly after the mad dream had passed.

Imlay was much away from Mary at first under the pretext of business. He would not be an American to neglect his love for business. His travels brought him, as the Germans say, to other cities and other loves. As a man that was his right, equally so was it his right to deceive Mary. What she must have endured only those can appreciate who have themselves known the tempest.

All through her pregnancy with Imlay's child, Mary pined for the man, begged and called, but he was busy. The poor chap did not know that all the wealth in the world could not make up for the wealth of Mary's love. The only consolation she found was in her work. She wrote *The French Revolution* right under the very influence of that tremendous drama. Keen as she was in her observation, she saw deeper than Burke, beneath all the terrible loss of life, she saw the still more terrible contrast between poverty and riches and [that] all the bloodshed was in vain so long as that contrast continued. Thus she wrote:

"If the aristocracy of birth is leveled with the ground only to make room for that of riches, I am afraid that the morale of the people will not be much improved by the change. Everything whispers to me that names, not principles, are changed."

She realized while in Paris what she had predicted in her attack on Burke, that the demon of property has ever been at hand to encroach on the sacred rights of man.

With all her work Mary could not forget her love. It was after a vain and bitter struggle to bring Imlay to her that she attempted suicide. She failed, and to get back her strength she went to Norway on a mission for Imlay. She recuperated physically, but her soul was bruised and scarred. Mary and Imlay came together several times, but it was only dragging out the inevitable. Then came the final blow. Mary learned that Imlay had other affairs and that he had been deceiving her, not so much out of mischief as out of cowardice.

She then took the most terrible and desperate step, she threw herself into the Thames after walking for hours to get her clothing wet [so] that she may surely drown. Oh, the inconsistencies, cry the superficial critics. But was it?

In the struggle between her intellect and her passion Mary had suffered a defeat. She was too proud and too strong to survive such a terrible blow. What else was there for her but to die?

Fate that had played so many pranks with Mary Wollstonecraft willed it otherwise. It brought her back to life and hope, only to kill her at their very doors.

She found in Godwin the first representative of Anarchist Communism, a sweet and tender camaraderie, not of the wild, primitive kind but the quiet, mature, warm sort, that soothes one like a cold hand upon a burning forehead. With him she lived consistently with her ideas in freedom, each apart from the other, sharing what they could of each other.

Again Mary was about to become a mother, not in stress and pain as the first time, but in peace and surrounded by kindness. Yet so strange is fate, that Mary had to pay with her life for the life of her little girl, Mary Godwin. She died on September tenth, 1797, barely thirty-eight years of age. Her confinement with the first child, though under the most trying of circumstances, was mere play, or as she wrote to her sister, "an excuse for staying in bed." Yet that tragic time demanded its victim. Fannie Imlay died of the death her mother failed to find. She committed suicide by drowning, while Mary Wollstonecraft Godwin became the wife of the sweetest lark of liberty, Shelley.

Mary Wollstonecraft, the intellectual genius, the daring fighter of the eighteenth, nineteenth, and twentieth Centuries, Mary Wollstonecraft, the woman and lover, was doomed to pain because of the very wealth of her being. With all her affairs she yet was pretty much alone, as every great soul must be alone—no doubt, that is the penalty for greatness.

Her indomitable courage in behalf of the disinherited of the earth has alienated her from her own time and created the discord in her being which alone accounts for her terrible tragedy with Imlay. Mary Wollstonecraft aimed for the highest summit of human possibilities. She was too wise and too worldly not to see the discrepancy between her world of ideals and her world of love that caused the break of the string of her delicate, complicated soul.

Perhaps it was best for her to die at that particular moment. For he who has ever tasted the madness of life can never again adjust himself to an even tenor. But we have lost much and can only be reconciled by what she has left, and that is much. Had Mary Wollstonecraft not written a line, her life would have furnished food for thought. But she has given both, she therefore stands among the world's greatest, a life so deep, so rich, so exquisitely beautiful in her complete humanity.

■ JEALOUSY: CAUSES AND A POSSIBLE CURE

[CA. 1912]

No one at all capable of an intense conscious inner life need ever hope to escape mental anguish and suffering. Sorrow and often despair over the so-called eternal fitness of things are the most persistent companions of our life. But they do not come upon us from the outside, through the evil deeds of particularly evil people. They are conditioned in our very being; indeed, they are interwoven through a thousand tender and coarse threads with our existence.

It is absolutely necessary that we realize this fact, because people who never get away from the notion that their misfortune is due to the wickedness of their fellows never can outgrow the petty hatred and malice which constantly blames, condemns, and hounds others for something that is inevitable as part of themselves. Such people will not rise to the lofty heights of the true humanitarian to whom good and evil, moral and immoral, are but limited terms for the inner play of human emotions upon the human sea of life.

The "beyond good and evil" philosopher, Nietzsche, is at present denounced as the perpetrator of national hatred and machine gun destruction; but only bad readers and bad pupils interpret him so. "Beyond good and evil" means beyond prosecution, beyond judging, beyond killing, etc. *Beyond Good and Evil* opens before our eyes a vista the background of which is individual assertion combined with the understanding of all others who are unlike ourselves, who are different.

By that I do not mean the clumsy attempt of democracy to regular the complexities of human character by means of external equality. The vision of "beyond good and evil" points to the right to oneself, to one's personality. Such possibilities do not exclude pain over the chaos of life, but they do exclude the puritanic righteousness that sits in judgment on all others except oneself.

It is self-evident that the thoroughgoing radical—there are many half-baked ones, you know—must apply this deep, humane recognition to the sex and love relation. Sex emotions and love are among the most intimate, the most intense and sensitive, expressions of our being. They are so deeply related to individual physical and psychic traits as to stamp each love affair an independent affair, unlike any other love affair. In other words, each love is the result of the impressions and characteristics the two people involved give to it. Every love relation should by its very nature remain an absolutely private affair. Neither the State, the Church, morality, or people should meddle with it.

Unfortunately this is not the case. The most intimate relation is subject to proscriptions, regulations, and coercions, yet these external factors are absolutely alien to love, and as such lead to everlasting contradictions and conflict between love and law.

The result of it is that our love life is merged into corruption and degradation. "Pure love," so much hailed by the poets, is in the present matrimonial, divorce, and alienation wrangles, a rare specimen indeed. With money, social standing, and position as the criteria for love, prostitution is quite inevitable, even if it be covered with the mantle of legitimacy and morality.

The most prevalent evil of our mutilated love-life is jealousy, often described as the "green-eyed monster" who lies, cheats, betrays, and kills. The popular notion is that jealousy is inborn and therefore can never be eradicated from the human heart. This idea is a convenient excuse for those who lack ability and willingness to delve into cause and effect.

Anguish over a lost love, over the broken thread of love's continuity, is indeed inherent in our very beings. Emotional sorrow has inspired many sublime lyrics, much profound insight and poetic exultation of a Byron, Shelley, Heine, and their kind. But will anyone compare this grief with what commonly passes as jealousy? They are as unlike as wisdom and stupidity. As refinement and coarseness. As dignity and brutal coercion. Jealousy is the very reverse of understanding, of sympathy, and of generous feeling. Never has jealousy added to character, never does it make the individual big and fine. What it really does is to make him blind with fury, petty with suspicion, and harsh with envy.

Jealousy, the contortions of which we see in the matrimonial tragedies and comedies, is invariably a one-sided, bigoted accuser, convinced of his own righteousness and the meanness, cruelty, and guilt of his victim. Jealousy does not even attempt to understand. Its one desire is to punish, and to punish as severely as possible. This notion is embodied in the code of honor, as represented in dueling or the unwritten law. A code which will have it that the seduction of a woman must be atoned with the death of the seducer. Even where seduction has not taken place, where both have voluntarily yielded to the innermost urge, honor is restored only when blood has been shed, either that of the man or the woman.

Jealousy is obsessed by the sense of possession and vengeance. It is quite in accord with all other punitive laws upon the statutes which still adhere to the barbarous notion that an offence, often merely the result of social wrongs, must be adequately punished or revenged.

A very strong argument against jealousy is to be found in the data of historians like Morgan, Reclus, and others, as to the sex relations among primitive people. Anyone at all conversant with their works knows that monogamy is a much later sex from which came into being as a result of the domestication and ownership of women, and which created sex monopoly and the inevitable feeling of jealousy.

In the past, when men and women intermingled freely without interference of law and morality, there could be no jealousy, because the latter rests upon the assumption that a certain man has an exclusive sex monopoly over a certain woman and *vice-versa*. The moment anyone dates to trespass this sacred precept, jealousy is up in arms. Under such circumstances it is ridiculous to say that jealousy is perfectly natural. As a matter of fact, it is the artificial result of an artificial cause, nothing else.

Unfortunately, it is not only conservative marriages which are saturated with the notion of sex monopoly; the so-called free unions are also victims of it. The argument may be raised that this is one more proof that jealousy is an inborn trait. But it must be borne in mind that sex monopoly has been handed down from generation to generation as a sacred right and the basis of purity of the family and the home. And just as the Church and the State accepted sex monopoly as the only security to the marriage tie, so have both justified jealousy as the legitimate weapon of defense for the protection of the property right.

Now, while it is true that a great many people have outgrown the legality of sex monopoly, they have not outgrown its traditions and habits. Therefore they become as blinded by the "green-eyed monster" as their conservative neighbors the moment their possessions are at stake.

A man or woman free and big enough not to interfere or fuss over the outside attractions of the loved one is sure to be despised by his conservative, and ridiculed by his radical, friends. He will either be decried as a degenerate or a coward; often enough some petty material motives will be imputed to him. In any even, such men and women will be the target of coarse gossip or filthy jokes for no other reason than that they concede to wife, husband or lovers the right to their own bodies and their emotional expression, without making jealous scenes or wild threats to kill the intruder.

There are other factors in jealousy: the conceit of the male and the envy of the female. The male in matters sexual is an imposter, a braggart, who forever boasts of his exploits and success with women. He insists on playing the part of a conqueror, since he has been told that women want to be conquered, that they love to be seduced. Feeling himself the only cock in the barnyard, or the bull who must clash horns in order to win the cow, he feels mortally wounded in his conceit and arrogance the moment a rival appears on the scene—the scene, even among so-called refined men, continues to be woman's sex love, which must belong to only one master.

In other words, the endangered sex monopoly together with man's outraged vanity in ninety-nine cases out of a hundred are the antecedents of jealousy.

In the case of a woman, economic fear for herself and children and her petty envy of every other woman who gains grace in the eyes of her supporter invariably create jealousy. In justice to women be it said that for centuries past, physical attraction was her only stock in trade, therefore she must needs become envious of the charm and value of other women as threatening her hold upon her precious property.

The grotesque aspect of the whole matter is that men and women often grow violently jealous of those they really do not care much about. It is therefore not their outraged love, but their outraged conceit and envy which cry out against this "terrible wrong." Likely as not the woman never loved the man whom she now suspects and spies upon. Likely as not she never made an effort to keep his love. But the moment a competitor arrives, she begins to value her sex property for the defense of which no means are too despicable or cruel.

Obviously, then, jealousy is not the result of love. In fact, if it were possible to investigate most cases of jealousy, it would likely be found that the less people are imbued with a great love the more violent and contemptible is their jealousy. Two people bound by inner harmony and oneness are not afraid to impair their mutual confidence and security if one or the other has outside attractions, nor will their relations end in vile enmity, as is too often the case with many people. They may not be able, nor ought they to be expected, to receive the choice of the loved one into the intimacy of their lives, but that does not give either one the right to deny the necessity of the attraction.

As I shall discuss variety and monogamy two weeks from tonight, I will not dwell upon either here, except to say that to look upon people who can love more than one person as perverse or abnormal is to be very ignorant indeed. I have already discussed a number of causes for jealousy to which I must add the institution of marriage which the State and Church proclaim as "the bond until death doth part." This is accepted as the ethical mode of right living and right doing.

With love, in all its variability and changeability, fettered and cramped, it is small wonder if jealousy arises out of it. What else but pettiness, meanness, suspicion, and rancor can come when a man and wife are officially held together with the formula "from now on you are one in body and spirit." Just take any couple tied together in such a manner, dependent upon each other for every thought and feeling, without an outside interest or desire, and ask yourself whether such a relation must not become hateful and unbearable in time.

In some form or other the fetters are broken, and as the circumstances which bring this about are usually low and degrading, it is hardly surprising that they bring into play the shabbiest and meanest human traits and motives.

In other words, legal, religious, and moral interference are the parents of our present unnatural love and sex life, and out of it jealousy has grown. It is the lash which whips and tortures poor mortals because of their stupidity, ignorance, and prejudice.

But no one need attempt to justify himself on the ground of being a victim of these conditions. It is only too true that we all smart under the burdens of iniquitous social arrangements, under coercion and moral blindness. But are we not conscious individuals, whose aim it is to bring truth and justice into human affairs? The theory that man is a product of conditions has led only to indifference and to a sluggish acquiescence in these conditions. Yet everyone knows that adaptation to an unhealthy and unjust mode of life only strengthens both, while man, the so-called crown of all creation, equipped with a capacity to think and see and above all to employ his powers of initiative, grows ever weaker, more passive, more fatalistic.

There is nothing more terrible and fatal than to dig into the vitals of one's loved ones and oneself. It can only help to tear whatever slender threads of affection still inhere in the relation and finally bring us to the last ditch, which jealousy attempts to prevent, namely, the annihilation of love, friendship and respect.

Jealousy is indeed a poor medium to secure love, but it is a secure medium to destroy one's self-respect. For jealous people, like dope-fiends, stoop to the lowest level and in the end inspire only disgust and loathing.

Anguish over the loss of love or a nonreciprocated love among people who are capable of high and fine thoughts will never make a person coarse. Those who are sensitive and fine have only to ask themselves whether they can tolerate any obligatory relation, and an emphatic *no* would be the reply. But most people continue to live near each other although they have long ceased to live with each other—a life fertile enough for the operation of jealousy, whose methods go all the way from opening private correspondence to murder. Compared with such horrors, open adultery seems an act of courage and liberation.

A strong shield against the vulgarity of jealousy is that man and wife are not of one body and one spirit. They are two human beings, of different temperament, feelings, and emotions. Each is a small cosmos in himself, engrossed in his own thoughts and ideas. It is glorious and poetic if these two worlds meet in freedom and equality. Even if this lasts but a short time it is already worthwhile. But, the moment the two worlds are forced together all the beauty and fragrance ceases and nothing but dead leaves remain. Whoever grasps this truism will consider jealousy beneath him and will not permit it to hang as a sword of Damocles over him.

All lovers do well to leave the doors of their love wide open. When love can go and come without fear of meeting a watch-dog, jealousy will rarely take root because it will soon learn that where there are no locks and keys there is no place for suspicion and distrust, two elements upon which jealousy thrives and prospers.

■ VICTIMS OF MORALITY

(1913)

Not so very long ago I attended a meeting addressed by Anthony Comstock, who has for forty years been the guardian of American morals. A more incoherent, ignorant ramble I have never heard from any platform.

The question that presented itself to me, listening to the commonplace, bigoted talk of the man, was, How could anyone so limited and unintelligent wield the power of censor and dictator over a supposedly democratic nation? True, Comstock has the law to back him. Forty years ago, when Puritanism was even more rampant than to-day, completely shutting out the light of reason and progress, Comstock succeeded, through shady machination and political wire pulling, to introduce a bill which gave him complete control over the Post Office Department—a control which has proved disastrous to the freedom of the press, as well as the right of privacy of the American citizen.

Since then, Comstock has broken into the private chambers of people, has confiscated personal correspondence, as well as works of art, and has established a system of espionage and graft which would put Russia to shame. Yet the law does not explain the power of Anthony Comstock. There is something else, more terrible than the law. It is the narrow puritanic spirit, as represented in the sterile minds of the Young-Men-and-Old-Maid's Christian Union, Temperance Union, Sabbath Union, Purity League, etc. A spirit which is absolutely blind to the simplest manifestations of life; hence stands for stagnation and decay. As in antebellum days, these old fossils lament the terrible immorality of our time. Science, art, literature, the drama, are at the mercy of bigoted censorship and legal procedure, with the result that America, with all her boastful claims to progress and liberty is still steeped in the densest provincialism.

The smallest dominion in Europe can boast of an art free from the fetters of morality, an art that has the courage to portray the great social problems of our time. With the sharp edge of critical analysis, it cuts into every social ulcer, every wrong, demanding fundamental changes and the transvaluation of accepted values.

Satire, wit, humor, as well as the most intensely serious modes of expression, are being employed to lay bare our conventional social and moral lies. In America we would seek in vain for such a medium, since even the attempt at it is made impossible by the rigid regime, by the moral dictator and his clique.

The nearest approach, however, are our muckrakers, who have no doubt rendered great service along economic and social lines. Whether the muckrakers have or have not helped to change conditions, at least they have torn the mask from the lying face of our smug and self-satisfied society.

Unfortunately, the Lie of Morality still stalks about in fine feathers, since no one dares to come within hailing distance of that holy of holies. Yet it is safe to say that no other superstition is so detrimental to growth, so enervating and paralyzing to the minds and hearts of the people, as the superstition of Morality.

The most pathetic, and in a way discouraging, aspect of the situation is a certain element of liberals, and even of radicals, men and women apparently free from religious and social spooks. But before the monster of Morality they are as prostrate as the most pious of their kind—which is an additional proof to the extent to which the morality worm has eaten into the system of its victims and how far-going and thorough the measures must be which are to drive it out again.

Needless to say, society is obsessed by more than one morality. Indeed, every institution of to-day has its own moral standard. Nor could they ever have maintained themselves, were it not for religion, which acts as a shield, and for morality, which acts as the mask. This explains the interest of the exploiting rich in religion and morality. The rich preach, foster, and finance both, as an investment that pays good returns. Through the medium of religion they have paralyzed the mind of the people, just as morality has enslaved the spirit. In other words, religion and morality are a much better whip to keep people in submission, than even the club and the gun.

To illustrate: The Property Morality declares that that institution is sacred. Woe to anyone that dares to question the sanctity of property, or sins against it! Yet everyone knows that Property is robbery; that it represents the accumulated efforts of millions, who themselves are propertyless. And what is more terrible, the more poverty stricken the victim of Property Morality is, the greater his respect and awe for that master. Thus we hear advanced people, even so-called class-conscious workingmen, decry as immoral such methods as sabotage and direct action, because they aim at Property. Verily, if the victims themselves are so blinded by the Property Morality, what need one expect from the masters? It therefore seems high time to bring home the fact that until the workers will lose respect for the instrument of their material enslavement, they need hope for no relief.

However, it is with the effect of Morality upon women that I am here mostly concerned. So disastrous, so paralyzing has this effect been, that some even of the most advanced among my sisters never thoroughly outgrow it.

It is Morality which condemns woman to the position of a celibate, a prostitute, or a reckless, incessant breeder of hapless children.

First, as to the celibate, the famished and withered human plant. When still a young, beautiful flower, she falls in love with a respectable young man. But Morality decrees that unless he can marry the girl, she must never know the raptures of love, the ecstasy of passion, which reaches its culminating expression in the sex embrace. The respectable young man is willing to marry, but the Property Morality, the Family and Social Moralities decree that he must first make his pile, must save up enough to establish a home and be able to provide for a family. The young people must wait, often many long, weary years.

Meanwhile the respectable young man, excited through the daily association and contact with his sweetheart, seeks an outlet for his nature in return for money. In ninety-nine cases out of a hundred, he will be infected, and when he is materially able to marry, he will infect his wife and possible offspring. And the young flower, with every fiber aglow with the fire of life, with all her being crying out for love and passion? She has no outlet. She develops headaches, insomnia, hysteria; grows embittered, quarrelsome, and soon becomes a faded, withered, joyless being, a nuisance to herself and everyone else. No wonder Stirner preferred the grisette to the maiden grown gray with virtue.

There is nothing more pathetic, nothing more terrible, than this gray-grown victim of a gray-grown Morality. This applies even with greater force to the masses of professional middle-class girls, than to those of the people. Through economic necessity the latter are thrust into life's jungle at an early age; they grow up with their male companions in the factory and shop, or at play and dance. The result is a more normal, expression of their physical instincts. Then too, the young men and women of the people are not so hide-bound by externalities, and often follow the call of love and passion regardless of ceremony and tradition.

But the overwrought and oversexed middle class girl, hedged in her narrow confines with family and social traditions, guarded by a thousand eyes, afraid of her own shadow—the yearning of her inmost being for the man or the child, must turn to cats, dogs, canary birds, or the Bible Class. Such is the cruel dictum of Morality, which is daily shutting out love, light, and joy from the lives of innumerable victims.

Now, as to the prostitute. In spite of laws, ordinances, persecution, and prisons; in spite of segregation, registration, vice crusades, and other similar devices, the prostitute is the real specter of our age. She sweeps across the plains like a fire burning into every nook of life, devastating, destroying.

After all, she is paying back, in a very small measure, the curse and horrors society has strewn in her path. She, weary with the tramp of ages, harassed and driven from pillar to post, at the mercy of all, is yet the Nemesis of modern times, the avenging angel, ruthlessly wielding the sword of fire. For has she not the man in her power? And, through him, the home, the child, the race. Thus she slays, and is herself the most brutally slain. What has made her? Whence does she come? Morality, the morality which is merciless in its attitude to women. Once she dared to be herself, to be true to her nature, to life, there is no return: the woman is thrust out from the pale and protection of society. The prostitute becomes the victim of Morality, even as the withered old maid is its victim. But the prostitute is victimized by still other forces, foremost among them the Property Morality, which compels woman to sell herself as a sex commodity for a dollar per, out of wedlock, or for fifteen dollars a week, in the sacred fold of matrimony. The latter is no doubt safer, more respected, more recognized, but of the two forms of prostitution the girl of the street is the least hypocritical, the least debased, since her trade lacks the pious mask of hypocrisy; and yet she is hounded, fleeced, outraged, and shunned, by the very powers that have made her: the financier, the priest, the moralist, the judge, the jailor, and the detective, not to forget her sheltered, respectably virtuous sister, who is the most relentless and brutal in her persecution of the prostitute.

Morality and its victim, the mother—what a terrible picture! Is there indeed anything more terrible, more criminal, than our glorified sacred function of motherhood? The woman, physically and mentally unfit to be a mother, yet condemned to breed; the woman, economically taxed to the very last spark of energy, yet forced to breed; the woman, tied to a man she loathes, whose very sight fills her with horror, yet made to breed; the woman, worn and used-up from the process of procreation, yet coerced to breed, more, ever more. What a hideous thing, this much-lauded motherhood! No wonder thousands of women risk mutilation, and prefer even death to this curse of the cruel imposition of the spook of Morality. Five thousand are yearly sacrificed upon the altar of this monster, that will not stand for prevention but would cure abortions. Five thousand soldiers in the battle for their physical and spiritual freedom, and as many thousands more who are crippled and mutilated rather than bring forth life in a society based on decay and destruction.

Is it because the modern woman wants to shirk responsibility, or that she lacks love for her offspring, that drives her to the most drastic and dangerous means to avoid bearing children? Only shallow, bigoted minds can bring such an accusation. Else they would know that the modern woman has become race conscious, sensitive to the needs and rights of the child, as the unit of the race, and that therefore the modern woman has a sense of responsibility and humanity, which was quite foreign to her grandmother.

With the economic war raging all around her, with strife, misery, crime, disease, and insanity staring her in the face, with numberless little children ground into gold dust, how can the self and race-conscious woman become a mother? Morality can not answer this question. It can only dictate, coerce, or condemn—and how many women are strong enough to face this condemnation, to defy the moral dicta? Few, indeed. Hence they fill the factories, the reformatories, the homes for feeble minded, the prisons, the insane asylums, or they die in the attempt to prevent child-birth. Oh, Motherhood, what crimes are committed in thy name! What hosts are laid at your feet, Morality, destroyer of life!

Fortunately, the Dawn is emerging from the chaos and darkness. Woman is awakening, she is throwing off the nightmare of Morality; she will no longer be bound. In her love for the man she is not concerned in the contents of his pocketbook, but in the wealth of his nature, which alone is the fountain of life and of joy. Nor does she need the sanction of the State. Her love is sanction enough for her. Thus she can abandon herself to the man of her choice, as the flowers abandon themselves to dew and light, in freedom, beauty, and ecstasy.

Through her re-born consciousness as a unit, a personality, a race builder, she will become a mother only if she desires the child, and if she can give to the child, even before its birth, all that her nature and intellect can yield: harmony, health, comfort, beauty, and, above all, understanding, reverence, and love, which is the only fertile soil for new life, a new being.

Morality has no terrors for her who has risen beyond good and evil. And though Morality may continue to devour its victims, it is utterly powerless in the face of the modern spirit, that shines in all its glory upon the brow of man and woman, liberated and unafraid.

■ THE SOCIAL ASPECTS OF BIRTH CONTROL

(1916)

It has been suggested that to create one genius nature uses all of her resources and takes a hundred years for her difficult task. If that be true, it takes nature even longer to create a great idea. After all, in creating a genius nature concentrates on one personality whereas an idea must eventually become the heritage of the race and must needs be more difficult to mould.

It is just one hundred and fifty years ago when a great man conceived a great idea, Robert Thomas Malthus, the father of Birth Control. That it should have taken so long a time for the human race to realize the greatness of that idea, is only one more proof of the sluggishness of the human mind. It is not possible to go into a detailed discussion of the merits of Malthus' contention, to wit, that the earth is not fertile or rich enough to supply the needs of an excessive race. Certainly if we will look across to the trenches and battlefields of Europe we will find that in a measure his premise was correct. But I feel confident that if Malthus would live to-day he would agree with all social students and revolutionists that if the masses of people continue to be poor and the rich grow ever richer, it is not because the earth is lacking in fertility and richness to supply the need even of an excessive race, but because the earth is monopolized in the hands of the few to the exclusion of the many.

Capitalism, which was in its baby's shoes during Malthus' time has since grown into a huge insatiable monster. It roars through its whistle and machine, "Send your children on to me, I will twist their bones; I will sap their blood, I will rob them of their bloom," for capitalism has an insatiable appetite.

And through its destructive machinery, militarism, capitalism proclaims, "Send your sons on to me, I will drill and discipline them until all humanity has been ground out of them; until they become automatons ready to shoot and kill at the behest of their masters." Capitalism cannot do without militarism and since the masses of people furnish the material to be destroyed in the trenches and on the battlefield, capitalism must have a large race.

In so called good times, capitalism swallows masses of people to throw them out again in times of "industrial depression." This superfluous human mass, which is swelling the ranks of the unemployed and which represents the greatest menace in modern times, is called by our bourgeois political economists the labor margin. They will have it that under no circumstances must the labor margin diminish, else the sacred institution known as capitalistic civilization will be undermined. And so the political economists, together with all sponsors of the capitalistic regime, are in favor of a large and excessive race and are therefore opposed to Birth Control.

Nevertheless Malthus' theory contains much more truth than fiction. In its modern aspect it rests no longer upon speculation, but on other factors which are related to and interwoven with the tremendous social changes going on everywhere.

First, there is the scientific aspect, the contention on the part of the most eminent men of science who tell us that an overworked and underfed vitality cannot reproduce healthy progeny. Beside the contention of scientists, we are confronted with the terrible fact which is now even recognized by benighted people, namely, that an indiscriminate and incessant breeding on the part of the over-worked and underfed masses has resulted in an increase of defective, crippled and unfortunate children. So alarming is this fact, that it has awakened social reformers to the necessity of a mental clearing house where the cause and effect of the increase of crippled, deaf, dumb and blind children may be ascertained. Knowing as we do that reformers accept the truth when it has become apparent to the dullest in society, there need be no discussion any longer in regard to the results of indiscriminate breeding.

Secondly, there is the mental awakening of woman, that plays no small part in behalf of Birth Control. For ages she has carried her burdens. Has done her duty a thousand fold more than the soldier on the battlefield. After all, the soldier's business is to take life. For that he is paid by the State, eulogized by political charlatans and upheld by public hysteria. But woman's function is to give life, yet neither the state nor politicians nor public opinion have ever made the slightest provision in return for the life woman has given.

For ages she has been on her knees before the altar of duty as imposed by God, by Capitalism, by the State, and by Morality. To-day she has awakened from her age-long sleep. She has shaken herself free from the nightmare of the past; she has turned her face towards the light and its proclaiming in a clarion voice that she will no longer be a party to the crime of bringing hapless children into the world only to be ground into dust by the wheel of capitalism and to be torn into shreds in trenches and battlefields. And who is to say her nay? After all it is woman who is risking her health and sacrificing her youth in the reproduction of the race. Surely she ought to be in a position to decide how many children she should bring into the world, whether they should be brought into the world by the man she loves and because she wants the child, or should be born in hatred and loathing.

Furthermore, it is conceded by earnest physicians that constant reproduction on the part of women has resulted in what the laity terms, "female troubles": a lucrative condition for unscrupulous medical men. But what possible reason has woman to exhaust her system in everlasting child bearing?

It is precisely for this reason that women should have the knowledge that would enable her to recuperate during a period of from three to five years between each pregnancy, which alone would give her physical and mental well-being and the opportunity to take better care of the children already in existence.

But it is not woman alone who is beginning to realize the importance of Birth Control. Men, too, especially working men, have learned to see in large families a millstone around their necks, deliberately imposed upon them by the reactionary forces in society because a large family paralyzes the brain and benumbs the muscles of the masses of working men. Nothing so binds the workers to the block as a brood of children and that is exactly what the opponents of Birth Control want. Wretched as the earnings of a man with a large family are, he cannot risk even that little, so he continues in the rut, compromises and cringes before his master, just to earn barely enough to feed the many little mouths. He dare not join a revolutionary organization; he dare not go on strike; he dare not express an opinion. Masses of workers have awakened to the necessity of Birth Control as a means of freeing themselves from the terrible yoke and still more as a means of being able to do something for those already in existence by preventing more children from coming into the world.

Last, but not least, a change in the relation of the sexes, though not embracing very large numbers of people, is still making itself felt among a very considerable minority. In the past and to a large extent with the average man to-day woman continues to be a mere object, a means to an end; largely a physical means and end. But there are men who want more than that from woman; who have come to realize that if every male were emancipated from the superstitions of the past nothing would yet be changed in the social structure so long as woman had not taken her place with him in the great social struggle. Slowly but surely these men have learned that if a woman wastes her substance in eternal pregnancies, confinements and diaper washing, she has little time left for anything else. Least of all has she time for the questions which absorb and stir the father of her children. Out of physical exhaustion and nervous stress she becomes the obstacle in the man's way and often his bitterest enemy. It is then for his own protection and also for his need of the companion and friend in the woman he loves that a great many men want her to be relieved from the terrible imposition of constant reproduction of life, that therefore they are in favor of Birth Control.

From whatever angle, then, the question of Birth Control may be considered, it is the most dominant issue of modern times and as such it cannot be driven back by persecution, imprisonment or a conspiracy of silence.

Those who oppose the Birth Control Movement claim to do so in behalf of motherhood. All the political charlatans prate about this wonderful motherhood, yet on closer examination we find that this motherhood has gone on for centuries past blindly and stupidly dedicating its offspring to Moloch. Besides, so long as mothers are compelled to work many hard hours in order to help support the creatures which they unwillingly brought into the world, the talk of motherhood is nothing else but cant. Ten per cent of married women in the city of New York have to help make a living. Most of them earn the very lucrative salary of $280 a year. How dare anyone speak of the beauties of Motherhood in the face of such a crime?

But even the better paid mothers, what of them? Not so long ago our old and hoary Board of Education declared that mother teachers may not continue to teach. Though these antiquated gentlemen were compelled by public opinion to reconsider their decision, it is absolutely certain that if the average teacher were to become a mother every year, she would soon lose her position. This is the lot of the married mother; what about the unmarried mother? Or is anyone in doubt that there are thousands of unmarried mothers? They crowd our shops and factories and industries everywhere, not by choice but by economic necessity. In their drab and monotonous existence the only color left is probably a sexual attraction which without methods of prevention invariably leads to abortions. Thousands of women are sacrificed as a result of abortions because they are undertaken by quack doctors, ignorant midwives in secrecy and in haste. Yet the poets and the politicians sing of motherhood. A greater crime was never perpetrated upon woman.

Our moralists know about it, yet they persist in behalf of an indiscriminate breeding of children. They tell us that to limit offspring is entirely a modern tendency because the modern woman is loose in her morals and wishes to shirk responsibility. In reply to this, it is necessary to point out that the tendency to limit offspring is as old as the race. We have as the authority for this contention an eminent German physician Dr. Theilhaber who has compiled historic data to prove that the tendency was prevalent among the Hebrews, the Egyptians, the Persians and many tribes of American Indians. The fear of the child was so great that the women used the most hideous methods rather than to bring an unwanted child into the world. Dr. Theilhaber enumerates fifty-seven methods. This data is of great importance in as much as it dispels the superstition that woman wants to become a mother of a large family.

No, it is not because woman is lacking in responsibility, but because she has too much of the latter that she demands to know how to prevent conception. Never in the history of the world has woman been so race conscious as she is to-day. Never before has she been able to see in the child, not only in her child, but every child, the unit of society, the channel through which man and woman must pass; the strongest factor in the building of a new world. It is for this reason that Birth Control rests upon such solid ground.

We are told that so long as the law on the statute books makes the discussion of preventives a crime, these preventives must not be discussed. In reply I wish to say that it is not the Birth Control Movement, but the law, which will have to go. After all, that is what laws are for, to be made and unmade. How dare they demand that life shall submit to them? Just because some ignorant bigot in his own limitation of mind and heart succeeded in passing a law at the time when men and women were in the thralls of religious and moral superstition, must we be bound by it for the rest of our lives? I readily understand why judges and jailers shall be bound by it. It means their livelihood; their function in society. But even judges sometimes progress. I call your attention to the decision given in behalf of the issue of Birth Control by Judge Gatens of Portland, Oregon. "It seems to me that the trouble with our people to-day is, that there is too much prudery. Ignorance and prudery have always been the millstones around the neck of progress. We all know that things are wrong in society; that we are suffering from many evils but we have not the nerve to get up and admit it, and when some person brings to our attention something we already know, we feign modesty and feel outraged." That certainly is the trouble with most of our law makers and with all those who are opposed to Birth Control.

I am to be tried at Special Sessions April 5th. I do not know what the outcome will be, and furthermore, I do not care. This dread of going to prison for one's ideas so prevalent among American radicals, is what makes the movement so pale and weak. I have no such dread. My revolutionary tradition is that those who are not willing to go to prison for their ideas have never been considered of much value to their ideas. Besides, there are worse places than prison. But whether I have to pay for my Birth Control activities or come out free, one thing is certain, the Birth Control movement cannot be stopped nor will I be stopped from carrying on Birth Control agitation. If I refrain from discussing methods, it is not because I am afraid of a second arrest, but because for the first time in the history of America, the issue of Birth Control through oral information is clear-cut and as I want it fought out on its merits, I do not wish to give the authorities an opportunity to obscure it by something else. However, I do want to point out the utter stupidity of the law. I have at hand the testimony given by the detectives, which, according to their statement, is an exact transcription of what I spelled for them from the platform. Yet so ignorant are these men that they have not a single contracept spelled correctly now.

It is perfectly within the law for the detectives to give testimony, but it is not within the law for me to read the testimony which resulted in my indictment. Can you blame me if I am an anarchist and have no use for laws? Also, I wish to point out the utter stupidity of the American court. Supposedly justice is to be meted out there. Supposedly there are to be no star chamber proceedings under democracy, yet the other day when the detectives gave their testimony, it had to be done in a whisper, close to the judge as at the confessional in a Catholic Church and under no circumstances were the ladies present permitted to hear anything that was going on. The farce of it all! And yet we are expected to respect it, to obey it, to submit to it.

I do not know how many of you are willing to do it, but I am not. I stand as one of the sponsors of a world-wide movement, a movement which aims to set woman free from the terrible yoke and bondage of enforced pregnancy; a movement which demands the right for every child to be well born; a movement which shall help free labor from its eternal dependence; a movement which shall usher into the world a new kind of motherhood. I consider this movement important and vital enough to defy all the laws upon the statute-books. I believe it will clear the way not merely for the free discussion of contracepts but for the freedom of expression in Life, Art and Labor, for the right of medical science to experiment with contracepts as it has in the treatment of tuberculosis or any other disease.

I may be arrested, I may be tried and thrown into jail, but I never will be silent; I never will acquiesce or submit to authority, nor will I make peace with a system which degrades woman to a mere incubator and which fattens on her innocent victims. I now and here declare war upon this system and shall not rest until the path has been cleared for a free motherhood and a healthy, joyous and happy childhood.

■ AGAIN THE BIRTH CONTROL AGITATION

(1916)

If any one is in doubt about the tremendous growth of the Birth Control movement, two recent happenings in New York City should dispel this doubt.

One is the opinion of Judge Wadhams of General Sessions, and the other is the desperate methods employed by the New York Police Department in dealing with the Birth Control advocates. Not only do the police arrest everyone who openly discusses or distributes Birth Control information, but they frame up charges against innocent victims. Of course, perjury is nothing new with the Police Department, so it may not surprise you to learn that the old staid method is again being used in the most flagrant manner,

First as to Judge Wadhams. A woman was brought before him for burglary. Mrs. Schnur declared that she was compelled to steal to obtain bread for her six children, the youngest of whom was ten months old.

Up until five years ago Samuel Schnur was able to support his family with his earnings as an operator on children's' coats in an east side shop. The close confinement ultimately had its effect on the man, and he developed tuberculosis. He kept at his work, despite his illness until discovered by an inspector of the Health Department, who refused to permit him to remain in the shop as long as he had the disease. Since that time he has been unable to obtain employment.

The burden of support fell on Mrs. Schnur, who has partially earned a living for the family by doing odd jobs. Recently she was unfortunate in obtaining employment, and quickly used up what little money she had on hand. Last month she entered the home of Morris Moskowitz, at 203 East Seventh Street, and stole a small sum of money and a watch, which resulted in her arrest.

In his opinion Judge Wadhams said that Mrs. Schnur had been found guilty on a previous occasion of theft, arising out of the same conditions, but sentence was suspended. Although the woman could be sentenced for a long term in prison, the Court said that the unusual circumstances were such as to warrant a further extension of clemency.

After discussing the condition of the husband and his inability to care for his family, Judge Wadhams made the following statement:

> Nevertheless he goes on becoming the father of children who have very little chance under the conditions to be anything else but tubercular, and, themselves growing up, to repeat the process with society. There is no law against that.
>
> But we have not only no birth regulation in such cases, but if information is given with respect to birth regulation people are brought to the bar of justice for it. There is a law they violate.

Judge Wadhams pointed out that many nations of Europe had adopted birth regulation with seemingly excellent results. He queried whether Americans had taken as common sense a view of the subject as we might.

"I believe," the Opinion continued, "that we are living in an age of ignorance which at some future time will be looked upon aghast as we look back upon conditions which we now permit to exist. So before us we have here a family increasing in number, with a tubercular husband, with a woman with a child at her breast, with other small children at her skirts, and no money."

It was certainly worth going to jail to teach a Judge the importance of Birth Control for the masses of people. However, even going to jail will never teach the police anything.

Friday, October 20th, I was subpoenaed to appear as a witness for Mr. Bolton Hall, in his trial before Special Sessions, Department Six, for having distributed Birth Control circulars at the Union Square meeting on May 20th. Mr. Hall was acquitted. Together with a number of friends, I left the court house about 5 P.M., and had barely gotten to the sidewalk when I was arrested by detective Price. When he was asked to show a warrant he said it was unnecessary, that I was in his charge and would have to come along. Knowing from the past that a detective, even like the Russian Black Hundred, is absolute, I went along to the Elizabeth Street station house, and was there placed under $1,000 bail for having distributed Birth Control leaflets at the Union Square meeting May 20th. Evidently the detectives took no heed to the overwhelming testimony brought to bear in behalf of Mr. Bolton Hall, a testimony which, of course, will also be brought to bear in my behalf, i. e., that neither Mr. Hall nor myself distributed Birth Control leaflets. The detectives had decided to engage in a frame-up and they straightway proceeded to carry out their decision.

You will recollect that last April, I was arrested for *having given out birth control information*; that I was tried and found guilty and that I preferred going to the Queen's County Jail rather than pay a fine of $100.00. With that in view it is hardly necessary for me to emphasize that I believe in the birth control issue, and that I believe in the necessity of giving people information. In other words, I am willing to take the consequences if I have been guilty of what the law pleases to call an offence, But, as it is, I have not given out the circulars and, of course, do not intend to be arrested and thrown into jail simply because the New York detectives want to crown themselves with laurels of stemming the tide of the Birth Control agitation.

Friday, October 27th, I appeared before Judge Barlow, a type out of Dickens or Victor Hugo. Hard, pompous and dull. I waived examination, and was held for trial.

I cannot say at present when the trial will come up, but I expect to get a postponement and probably secure a jury trial. Meanwhile I am out on $1,000 bail.

On October 30th three cases were tried in the Court of Special Sessions: Jesse Ashley and two I.W.W. boys, Kerr and Marman. Of course they were all found guilty. Jesse Ashley was sentenced to pay $50.00 fine or serve 10 days in jail. She would have preferred the jail sentence but was urged to make a test case. Therefore she paid the fine under protest and will appeal.

Kerr and Marman will probably fare worse, inasmuch as the detective testified that while speaking on Madison Square, the boys offered a Birth Control pamphlet for sale at 10 cents and gave away with it—Oh, horrors!—"Preparedness: The Road to Universal Slaughter," by E. G. Little did we dream, when we published the pamphlet what an important part it would play in a New York court.

The two boys insisted that what they did do was to sell the "preparedness" pamphlet and give the Birth Control leaflet gratis. But though judges know that detectives never hesitate to perjure themselves, Kerr and Marman were found guilty.

However; it was evident that the judges are being educated. Thus one of them was very emphatic in saying that he means to distinguish between those that give Birth Control information free, out of conviction, and those that sell it. No such instruction was made in either Bill Sanger's, Ben Reitman's, or my case, although none of us sold information.

The opinion of the judge, then, proves that direct action is the only action that counts. But for those of us who have defied the law, Birth Control would still be a parlor proposition, as it continues to be to this day with nearly all of the Birth Control leagues in this country.

■ THE WOMAN SUFFRAGE CHAMELEON

(1917)

For well-nigh half a century the leaders of woman suffrage have been claiming that miraculous results would follow the enfranchisement of woman. All the social and economic evils of past centuries would be abolished once woman will get the vote. All the wrongs and injustices, all the crimes and horrors of the ages would be eliminated from life by the magic decree of a scrap of paper.

When the attention of the leaders of the movement was called to the fact that such extravagant claims convince no one, they would say, "Wait until we have the opportunity; wait till we are face to face with a great test, and then you will see how superior woman is in her attitude toward social progress."

The intelligent opponents of woman suffrage, who were such on the ground that the representative system has served only to rob man of his independence, and that it will do the same to woman, knew that nowhere has woman suffrage exerted the slightest influence upon the social and economic life of the people. Still they were willing to give the suffrage exponents the benefit of doubt. They were ready to believe that the suffragists were sincere in their claim that woman will never be guilty of the stupidities and cruelties of man. Especially did they look to the militant suffragettes of England for a superior kind of womanhood. Did not Mrs. Emmeline Pankhurst make the bold statement from an American platform that woman is more humane than man, and that she never would be guilty of his crimes: for one thing, woman does not believe in war, and will never support wars.

But politicians remain politicians. No sooner did England join the war, for humanitarian reasons, of course, than the suffrage ladies immediately forgot all their boasts about woman's superiority and goodness and immolated their party on the altar of the very government which tore their clothing, pulled their hair and fed them forcibly for their militant activities. Mrs. Pankhurst and her hosts became more passionate in their war mania, in their thirst for the enemy's blood than the most hardened militarists. They consecrated their all, even their sex attraction, as a means of luring unwilling men into the military net, into the trenches and death. For all this they are now to be rewarded with the ballot. Even Asquith, the erstwhile foe of the Pankhurst outfit, is now convinced that woman ought to have the vote, since she has proven so ferocious in her hate, and is so persistently bent on conquest. All hail to the English women who bought their vote with the blood of the millions of men already sacrificed to the monster War. The price is indeed great, but so will be the political jobs in store for the lady politicians.

The American suffrage party, bereft of an original idea since the days of Elizabeth Cady Stanton, Lucy Stone, and Susan Anthony, must needs ape with parrot-like stupidity the example set by their English sisters. In the heroic days of militancy, Mrs. Pankhurst and her followers were roundly repudiated by the American suffrage party. The respectable, lady-like Mrs. Catt would have nothing to do with such ruffians as the militants. But when the suffragettes of England, with an eye for the flesh pots of Parliament, turned somersault, the American suffrage party followed suit. Indeed, Mrs. Catt did not even wait until war was actually declared by this country. She went Mrs. Pankhurst one better. She pledged her party to militarism, to the support of every autocratic measure of the government long before there was any necessity for it all. Why not? Why waste another fifty years lobbying for the vote if one can get it by the mere betrayal of an ideal? What are ideals among politicians, anyway!

The arguments of the antis that woman does not need the vote because she has a stronger weapon—her sex—was met with the declaration that the vote will free woman from the degrading need of sex appeal. How does this proud boast compare with the campaign started by the suffrage party to lure the manhood of America into the European sea-blood? Not only is every youth and man to be brazenly solicited and cajoled into enlisting by the fair members of the suffrage party, but wives and sweethearts are to be induced to play upon the emotions and feelings of the men, to bring their sacrifice to the Moloch of Patriotism and War.

How is this to be accomplished? Surely not by argument. If during the last fifty years the women politicians failed to convince most men that woman is entitled to political equality, they surely will not convince them suddenly that they ought to go to certain death while the women remain safely tucked away at home sewing bandages. No, not argument, reason or humanitarianism has the suffrage party pledged to the government; it is the sex attraction, the vulgar persuasive and ensnaring appeal of the female let loose for the glory of the country. What man can resist that? The greatest have been robbed of their sanity and judgment when benumbed by the sex appeal. How is the youth of America to withstand it?

The cat is out of the bag. The suffrage ladies have at last proven that their prerogative is neither intelligence nor sincerity, and that their boast of equality is all rot; that in the struggle for the vote, even, the sex appeal was their only resort, and cheap political reward their only aim. They are now using both to feed the cruel monster war, although they must know that awful as the price is which man pays, it is as naught compared with the cruelties, brutalities, and outrage woman is subjected to by war.

The crime which the leaders of the American woman suffrage party have committed against their constituency is in direct relation of the procurer to his victim. Most of them are too old to effect any result upon enlistment through their own sex appeal, or to render any personal service to their country. But in pledging the support of the party they are victimizing the younger members. This may sound harsh, but it is true nevertheless. Else how are we to explain the pledge, to make a house to house canvass, to work upon the patriotic hysteria of women, who in turn are to use their sex appeal upon the men to enlist. In other words, the very attribute woman was forced to use for her economic and social status in society, and which the suffrage ladies have always repudiated, is now to be exploited in the service of the Lord of War.

In justice to the Woman's Political Congressional Union and a few individual members of the suffrage party be it said that they have refused to be cajoled by the suffrage leaders. Unfortunately, the Woman's Political Congressional Union is really between and betwixt in its position. It is neither for war nor for peace. That was all well and good so long as the monster walked over Europe only. Now that it is spreading itself at home, the Congressional Union will find that silence is a sign of consent. Their refusal to come out determinedly against war practically makes them a party to it.

In all this muddle among the suffrage factions, it is refreshing indeed to find one woman decided and firm. Jannette Rankin's refusal to support the war will do more to bring woman nearer to emancipation than all political measures put together. For the present she is no doubt considered anathema, a traitor to her country. But that ought not to dismay Miss Rankin. All worth-while men and women have been decried as such. Yet they and not the loud mouthed, weak-kneed patriots are of value to posterity.

■ LOUISE MICHEL

[1923]*

Dear Dr. Hirschfeld:

I have been familiar with your great work on sex psychology for a number of years. I have admired the brave struggle you have made for the rights of people who, by their very nature, cannot find sex expression in what is commonly called "the normal way." And now that I have been fortunate enough to know you and see your efforts at close range, I am more than ever impressed with your personality and the spirit which has sustained you in your difficult task. Your readiness to give my refutation of Frhr. von Levetzow's appraisement of Louise Michel as an Urning proves, if proofs were needed, that you have a fine sense of justice which seeks only to ascertain the truth. I thank you for that and for the able and heroic stand you have taken against ignorance and hypocrisy on behalf of light and humanism.

Before I deal with the article, permit me to say this: it is not prejudice against homosexuality or the aversion to homosexuals which prompts me to point out the errors in the claim of the author. If Louise Michel had ever demonstrated homosexual traits to those who knew and loved her, I should be the last

---

* A draft of a letter addressed to Dr. Magnus Hirschfeld, editor of the *Jahrbuch für sexuelle Zwischenstufen* (Yearbook for Sexual Intermediates.) Karl von Levetzow's study of Louise Michel, which concluded that she was a lesbian, had appeared in 1906. The original can be consulted in the Emma Goldman Papers of the International Institute of Social History, Ms. 208. In this transcription, a few illegible corrections could not be included. Minor corrections have been made to punctuation and spelling, particularly in the case of proper names. —Ed.

person to attempt to clear her from the "stigma." I may, indeed, consider it a tragedy for those who are sexually differentiated in a world so bereft of understanding for the homosexual, or so ignorant of the meaning and importance of the whole gamut of sex. But I certainly do not think such people inferior, less moral, or less capable of following feelings and actions. Least of all should I consider it necessary to "clear" my illustrious teacher and comrade, Louise Michel, of the charge of homosexuality. Her value to humanity, or contribution to the emancipation of the slaves, is so great that nothing could add or detract from her, whatever her sexual gratification may have been.

Years ago, when I knew nothing at all about sex psychology, and when my only acquaintance with homosexuals were some of the women I had met in prison where I was incarcerated for my political opinions, I came out in defense of Oscar Wilde. As an Anarchist, my place has ever been with the persecuted. I saw in the persecution and prosecution of Oscar Wilde reflected the cruel injustice and hypocrisy of the very society which sent him to his doom. Hence my defense of him.

Later, I went to Europe, and there came upon the works of Havelock Ellis, Krafft-Ebbing, Carpenter, and many others, which made me see the crime against Oscar Wilde and his kind in a more glaring light. From that time on I used my pen and voice in behalf of those whom nature herself has destined to be different in their sex psychology and needs. Your works, Dear Doctor, have helped me much in shedding light on the very complex question of sex psychology, and in humanizing the attitude of people who came to hear me.

From this, your readers will see that I have no prejudice whatever, or the least antipathy, to homosexuals. Quite to the contrary. I have among my friends men and women either complete Urnings or Bi-Sexuals. I have found them far above the average in intelligence, ability, sensitiveness and charm. I feel deeply with them, because I know that their sufferings are greater and more complex than that of most people. There is, however, one predominant tendency among homosexuals which I must oppose. It is their attempt to claim every outstanding personality for their creed, to ascribe to them traits and characteristics inherent in themselves.

Now, it may be psychologically conditioned in all persecuted people to cling for support to the exceptional types of every period. Misery ever seeks companionship. Thus, for instance, the Jews will have it that most great men and women in the world have either been of Jewish origin or have Jewish characteristics. The Irish will do the same. The Hindus will tell you that their civilization is the greatest in the world and so on and so forth. It is the same with political outcasts. Socialists claim Walt Whitman and Oscar Wilde for the theories of Marx, while many Anarchists will point to Nietzsche, Wagner, Ibsen and others as to their very own. To be sure, greatness always goes with versatility, but I have always considered it an imposition to lay claim upon any great creative person for my ideas, unless he or she so claims themselves.

If one is to accept the contention of many homosexuals for granted, one would have to come to the conclusion that there was or cannot be greatness outside of sexually inverted people. Persecution breeds sectarianism; this, in return, makes people limited in their scope, and very often unfair in their appraisement of others. I rather think that Frhr. Karl von Levetzow suffers from an overdose of homosexual sectarianism. Added to this is his antiquated view towards the female. He sees in woman only the charmer of men, the bearer of children, and, in a more vulgar sense, the general cook and bottle-washer of the household. Any woman who lacks these time-worn requisites for femininity, the author will immediately claim as an Urning. In the light of modern woman's achievements in every domain of human thought and social endeavor, this view of the conventional male towards the female hardly merits a moment's consideration. Still, I shall have to deal with this hoary attitude of the author of "Louise Michel," if only to demonstrate the absurd conclusions one may come to if he starts from an absurd premise.

My criticism of von Levetzow does not prevent me from paying him tribute as a great literary artist and a man capable of sympathetic understanding of a great soul. In fact, I feel some-what guilty to have to dissect the article. It is as if I attempted to slice up a great, radiant portrait painted by a master hand, for von Levetzow's pen-picture of Louise Michel is a masterpiece. For that, all of us who knew and loved this marvelous woman, are greatly indebted to him. However, the truth demands that I set my own feelings aside and deal with facts.

To deal adequately with the points raised in the article it would necessitate to publish the text in full, together with my reply, or at least to quote at great length, and then take up each point in detail. That, however, would take up too much space of your valuable "Jahrbuch." I will, therefore, content myself with a mere gist of the salient points raised in proof of Louise Michel's homosexuality.

Now, what are these points?

First, Louise Michel was an exceptional child, eager for knowledge and scientific problems, and a vociferous reader. Second, her playthings, unlike those of other girls, were not dolls, but frogs, beetles, mice and other living things. Third, Louise Michel played with her cousin (by the way, this would prove that Louise was a perfectly normal girl, otherwise she would have chosen girls for her companions), climbed trees, inaugurated hunting expeditions, romped and was altogether full of boyish pranks and mischief. Fourth, she grew very indifferent to appearance, hated and opposed feminine frills, corsets, high heels and the rest, was terribly negligent about herself and disorderly in her habits and her surroundings. Fifth, Louise Michel was extraordinarily courageous, lacking in the element of fear, daring to the point of recklessness. Her power of endurance through physical suffering was hardly equaled by men. Sixth, no man had been in her life except as comrades. On the other hand, she was always surrounded "with passionately loved" women friends. Last, but not least, Louise Michel was a mathematician and a composer, loved sculpture, enthused over Wagner and did ever so many other things which women never have done. The author lays great stress on Louise Michel's angular figure, flatness of chest, and masculine features. In short, he brings forth every imaginable argument to prove the masculinity of Louise Michel, arguments used from time immemorial by all sorts of men against woman whenever she attempted to rise out of the position of the harem inmate, and tried to achieve an equal place in life with man.

Let us see how true all these so-called facts are.

First, the early proclivities of Louise Michel for the deep problems of life, her reading of serious books and her mathematical sense, have been part of the make-up of quite a number of great women; to mention only a few, Sofia Kovalevskaya, Marie Bashkirtseff, and, in modern times, Madame Curie. Kovalevskaya solved serious mathematical problems at the age of eight, and became, when she was barely twenty-five, one of the greatest mathematicians of the time. Bashkirtseff had a far deeper psychologic understanding for her surrounding than a great many men; she occupied herself with the study of science, sociology, literature, art, music, when she was ten years of age, and became one of the most remarkable figures of her time. Madame Curie is too well know, not merely as a help-mate of her husband, but as an independent authority in science.... Yet these women, and quite a number outside of them, were not only not homosexual, but were extremely feminine; this femininity was, to a large extent, the great tragedy in their lives, for the men they met were unable to grasp the yearning spirit of these women for the love and the comradeship of the man. Thus, Sofia Kovalevskaya wasted her substance with her husband, and later in a violent passion for a compatriot of hers who never suspected the flame that was consuming this great woman of the 19th century. I have no desire to go into the private life of Madame Curie. She probably would consider it an imposition; but as much as is known of her private life, she seems to be eminently feminine and have no homosexual proclivities whatsoever.

I am quite sure that Frhr. von Levetzow has never seen healthy, normal American girls at play. He would find that they can romp, climb trees, play with frogs, beetles and snakes, and do all sorts of so-called "boyish" things, and yet grow up to be very frivolous, typically feminine, and often useless women. On the other hand, there are any number of great American women, almost in every walk of life, who were very boyish in their childhood, and who yet are great lovers of men, mothers of children, and, at the same time, a great moral force in the different movements for deeper and finer social value in their country.

Louise Michel's courage, reckless daring, lack of fear, and power of physical endurance—certainly I will not gainsay her in all that. But it would be unfair to the great host of Russian revolutionary women if I were to emphasize all the wonderful traits of Louise without giving them credit for theirs. It is evident that the author of the article has never come across these women, to mention but a few: Perovskaya, Gelfman, Figner, Breskovskaya, Kovalskaya, Volkenstein, and of the later period, Spiridonova.† All these women have been heroic in the great revolutionary struggle of Russia. They committed the most daring deeds and went to their death or to the still greater calvary, Siberia and Katorga, with a smile on their face. Yet Perovskaya preferred to die at the gallows with her beloved husband rather than escape to safety which she could very easily have done. Gelfman and Figner were so eminently feminine that they suffered more from the lack of beauty and delicacy which goes to make up a sensitive woman's life than they did from the physical horrors of the prison. Kovalevskaya continued her rebellious struggle all though the years of imprisonment—something like twenty-two years. Volkenstein and Figner were among the most beautiful women, physically, feminine in their love life and in their associations. As to Spiridonova, she was subjected to the most fiendish tortures, including outrage by drunkard Russian officers; her naked body was burned with lighted cigars, but never a sound could be heard from her. Yet Spiridonova is a delicate and frail little

---

† Sophia Perovskaya, Gesya Gelfman, Vera Figner, Catherine Breshkovsky, Yelizaveta Kovalskaya, Ludmilla Volkenstein, and Maria Spiridonova. —Ed.

person, deeply in love with her comrade, and altogether so sensitive as a flower. These few examples should suffice to convince anyone not steeped in sectarianism or in the old threadworn notions of the nature of woman, of the fact that one can be very much of a woman and at the same time a great rebel and fighter. However, I might go on enumerating women in every country, every age and every clime, she stood side by side with the men in the great struggles for human right and for their own emancipation, who were certainly as brave and daring as their comrades, and yet had nothing whatever of masculinity or homosexuality in them.

This brings me to the absurd conclusion which von Levetzow draws from the tragic grandeur of the last meeting between Dombrovski and Louise Michel on the barricades.[‡] The author is so limited in his masculine conception of woman that he cannot understand how two such people, in the face of the collapse of the cause they loved more than life itself, would meet like comrades. He remarks "if Dombrovski had seen the woman in Louise, he would have patted her cheek; as it is he stretched out both his hands, and grasped hers in a last farewell." I am surprised that a man of von Levetzow's sensitiveness could be capable of such vulgarity. I rather think it is his ignorance of the wonderful relation which existed and still exist between men and women who are engaged in the fight for an ideal, or who have a common cause. It is true that very often the consciousness of the difference of sex is obliterated between them; they are comrades, capable of the highest sacrifice for each other and devotion to each other. Here again I would have to name every country and every clime that has given to the world such beautiful comradeship between men and women, but space will not permit. I merely raise this point to emphasize the absurdity of the arguments of the author on "Louise Michel."

---

‡General Jaroslav Dombrovski, commander-in-chief of the defense forces in the last days of the Paris Commune, killed on the barricades May 23, 1871. —Ed.

Louise Michel hated woman's frills and the rest of the requisite which go to make up the unfortunate hot-house plant of a perverted society, and that she was careless and disorderly. As far as the first so-called argument is concerned, I must enlighten von Levetzow. It is true that many women who have emancipated themselves from the shame of the past have also developed a new conception of beauty and fitness of attire. But in most cases, it was a just protest against the rags, the waste and the stupidity of the whole paraphernalia which went to make up the ordinary woman's outfit. From a scientific, a sociological and a moral point of view, these women have insisted that the mark of enslavement for their sex has been her clothes, and that she cannot really be free unless she transvalues the value of the things which held her to bondage. Are these women, therefore, homosexual? No more than Louise has been. Louise, who dedicated her life to the cause of humanity, who not only was engaged in the struggle for existence for her mother and herself, but was foremost in the movement which absorbed most of her thoughts and all her energies. Was she to spend her hours before the mirror, exploit dressmakers and torture salesgirls in a vain pursuit of the latest styles, and must she, therefore, be considered an Urning because she dressed sensibly and paid very little attention to what is commonly called the beauties of woman's appearance? Verily, if the author had no better proof for his claim, he should have refrained from making out his case.

Louise Michel has an angular figure; she had masculine features. It is not true, as the author will have it, that she had a masculine voice. I heard her speak when she was 66 years of age; her voice was a beautiful contralto, deep and melodious, and went straight to the heart of her hearers. With that was a remarkable simplicity which explains the great power she had over her audiences. As to her face, it is clear to me that von Levetzow never saw Louise smile. If he had done so he would no longer have seen the male in her. It is known to all who were close to Louise Michel what an illuminating effect her smile and her beautiful eyes created. This argument, too, seems very lame.

However, we come to the most important contention of von Levetzow. The author relates the fact that Louise repulsed two suitors because she was not attracted to men. It is significant, however, that this happened when she was 12 and 13 years of age, and the men were old enough to be her fathers; besides that, they came to buy her. She, herself, expresses her indignation and repulsion against such men, on page 330. Also her attitude towards the marriage institution is very significant (page 332). Louise resents marriage without love, as every self-respecting woman should. But nowhere in her writings has she expressed opposition to love without marriage. Nor has she ever written about the necessity of announcing from the housetops that so intimate and private an experience as the love life between two people should become common property. Proof for that is the following:

Louise Michel had a love experience with a teacher when she, herself, was quite a young girl, and was supporting herself as a teacher. Later, after her return from New Caledonia, she lived for a time with a Belgian comrade of hers. And if she did not have more experiences of that sort, it is probably because, as she herself stated, "I had given my heart to the Revolution." Yes, that was Louise's lover. All her life she was dedicated to that love. Types like Louise Michel can have no personal love which in any way interferes with their one great passion for an ideal, and Louise's passion for her ideal was the most overpowering element in her life, and went with her to her grave.

It is true she had a number of women friends whom she loved, not in the way von Levetzow will have it. A great many modern women who have little of the personal love in their lives, attach themselves in comradeship and devoted friendship with their own sex, just as great men do. The reason for that, in the case of the women, is that they find better understanding with members of their own sex than they do with the men of their time. The fact of the matter is that the modern man is still very much in the skin of his forebear,

Adam, not very much different in his attitude towards woman than the average man. On the other hand, the modern women is no longer satisfied with merely the lover; she wants understanding, comradeship, she wants to be treated as a human being, and not as an object for sex gratification. Since she cannot always find it in the man, she turns to her own sisters. It is precisely *because there is no sex element* between them that they can better understand each other. In other words, instead of being attracted to her woman friends by her homosexual tendencies, Louise was attracted to them because she was very much the woman, and needed the companionship of women. There is one more thing which was very prominent in Louise Michel; it was her mother instinct. She was passionately fond of children, mothered every waif she could pick up; it was her mother love which prompted her to adopt Charlotte Vauzelle, to bring her up and share with her out of her meager earnings. Never at any time was Charlotte even in the spiritual sense the sweetheart of Louise Michel. The fact of the matter is that Louise paid dearly for her devotion to Charlotte. The latter, together with her brother, made the last years of Louise Michel very miserable. They kept her a prisoner to a large extent, never letting her alone to receive her friends or to live with them. Charlotte opened Louise's mail and watched her constantly. The reason for it is that both Charlotte and her brother lived off Louise Michel and were mortally afraid that anyone else might benefit by the great generosity of Louise. In any event, it is ridiculous to point to Charlotte Vauzelle as the sweetheart of Louise Michel.

Louise Michel's love for sculpture and her appreciation of Wagner are brought forward as Uranian traits. Von Levetzow will have it that no woman is capable of creative art and music. He graciously admits that Francisco Holmés, the French-Scandinavian woman, was a great composer.[§] But he hastens to add that, according to her photograph, she looks masculine. I do not think that it is worth while to go into this

§ Perhaps Augusta Holmès, a French-Irish composer. —Ed.

argument. The fact that there were only a few great women composers does not make them homosexual. They are simply pioneers in the domain so far not explored by many women. As to the love of Wagner, the truth is that more women attend Wagnerian music and understand him than men. Perhaps it is because the elemental untrammeled spirit of Wagner's music affects the women as the releasing force of the pent-up and hidden emotions of their souls. It is hardly necessary to emphasize that women are not only capable of the appreciation of sculpture, but that there are quite a number of women sculptors of no small merit.

There is one thing in which I quite agree with von Levetzow: it is when he says that Louise Michel was so inseparably wound up with Anarchism that to grasp her personality and her complex nature, one must also go into a discussion of her social philosophy. But, as he justly says, the *Jahrbuch* is not the place to do so. But even if it were, I do not think that the author would have been in a position to undertake an analysis of Anarchism, since he seems to know absolutely nothing about it. Else, how is one to understand his interpretation on page 315 (line 4 to 7). What an insult to the memory of Louise Michel and the intelligence of the readers of the *Jahrbuch*!

I have known Louise Michel for a number of years. Long before I met her I knew her ideas and the price she had paid in the struggle for them. Her fortitude, her martyrdom, and more than that her boundless love for humanity, were to me like a purifying and illuminating flame. I met her the first time in 1896 in London; I was frequently with her then, and learned from her the story of the heroic struggle of the Paris Commune. Louise never spoke of herself and her own part in that struggle.

I met her again in 1899, in London, then in 1900, when for the first time in many years Louise Michel came back to Paris. It was during both periods that I had the opportunity to be much with her, and to receive from her a few snatches of her life, as it was my intention to write her biography. But she was so morbidly reticent about everything pertaining to herself that she was loath to discuss her own life. Always, however, she would become radiant, her face would light up by a divine fire when she would come to speak of others; her comrades, whom she nursed and cared for in New Caledonia; or, if she would speak of dumb creatures. For among other traits of Louise Michel was her great sympathy for animals. The little cottage she lived in in London was a perfect menagerie of stray cats and dogs that she picked up at night on her way home. Especially, her love for cats was certainly anything but masculine. It is true that von Levetzow relates the fact that Louise, standing on the barricades and surrounded by bullets, rescued a cat which had pressed close to the wall paralyzed with fright. History has never yet mentioned any man who, in time of danger, would do such a thing. I don't mean to say that he would not rescue a child or even a dog; but certainly never a cat.

The so-called masculine Louise Michel, who was disorderly, and could do nothing to keep herself tidy, in short, who was not domestic, yet learned to knit, darn, wash and cook for her fellow exiles in New Caledonia, besides nursing them with a tenderness of her great mother heart, and to keep up their spirit when the dreadful of their lives would overcome them.

I remember one wonderful evening in Paris. Anarchist friends of ours arranged a little dinner party for Louise and invited me to it. Louise, dressed in her usual black, with only a white lace collar and cuffs to give it relief, her face flushed like the roses on the table, and framed by her curly silvery hair, was radiant with the joy of being back in the city of her dreams and her struggles, and surrounded by intimate comrades. She was more talkative than I had ever heard her before, more willing to let us look into her soul. Never a moment did Louise show even the remotest masculine characteristic or homosexual tendencies. I am sure that they would not have escaped me had there been anything of that in Louise Michel for, as I said, in the beginning of my article, I have made a study of all the best literature on homosexuality, had known many homosexuals and easily detected homosexual leanings in people. There was no trace of that in Louise Michel.

But among the friends of Louise Michel are the greatest men of her time—Peter Kropotkin, Malatesta, Elisée Reclus, Malato, Rocker. Some of them lived close to her, were almost in daily contact. Had there been the slightest indication of homosexuality, they would have seen it; it would certainly have been known among her comrades. I have recently spoken to my friend and comrade, Rudolf Rocker, about this phase treated in the article of von Levetzow. He, too, assured me that never at any time has any one of the intimate friends of Louise Michel seen the slightest indication of homosexual leanings. I might say in passing that Rudolf Rocker, like myself, is perfectly free of any prejudice towards homosexuals. Our only desire is to prove Louise Michel as she really was—an exceptional woman, a great mind, and a wonderful spirit. She represented the new type of womanhood, yet as old as the race, as wise as time, and with a soul of an all-embracing and all-understanding love for mankind. In short, a complete woman, freed from the prejudice and the tradition which for centuries past have held woman in bondage and have condemned her to the position of a domestic and sexual slave. In Louise Michel there has risen the new woman who is capable of the most heroic deeds, yet at the same time remains the woman in her passion and love life.

Dear Dr. Hirschfeld, I have attempted in as concise a manner as possible, to analyze critically the contentions of Frhr. von Levetzow. You will agree with me, I am sure, that neither the question of homosexuality or of the homosexuals can gain anything by a misstatement of facts. For this reason, I have undertaken to prove the errors in the article, and for no other reason. I hope you will find my criticism convincing and that you will not only, as you have kindly offered, publish my reply, but will also take off the photograph of Louise Michel from your gallery of Urnings.

Faithfully,
Emma Goldman

■ EMMA'S LOVE VIEWS

(1926)

NOTE—No woman in modern time has been more actively hostile to the marriage custom than Emma Goldman, who, some eight years ago, was among a shipload of deportees sent back to Russia. She made lecture tours of America, speaking on marriage, and wrote pamphlets. Then, suddenly came word from Montreal, Can., that Emma Goldman had arrived under the name of Mrs. E. C. Colton. After a lifetime of antagonism, Emma Goldman herself had married a Welch miner. Her followers were amazed and still are. What could this mean? NEA sent a representative to locate her and learn at first hand what Emma Goldman now thinks of marriage. Herewith is presented an exclusive, personally written article, the second of a series of five, outlining her opinions today.

Many people have expressed surprise that I, who have for so many years criticized the marriage institution, should in the end have submitted to it.

Invariably they demand to know whether I have changed my view, held in the past.

I cannot be too emphatic in my declaration that now, as ever, I am convinced that the institution of marriage, as such, can add nothing whatever to the fundamental motives that bring men and women together. It will always be my feeling that the union of two people is an entirely private affair.

Bizarre Then—Accepted Now

Not many years ago this point of view was considered startling and revolutionary. Today it meets with far more general acceptance than some care to admit.

Even conservative people are beginning to realize that while marriage may be a matter of convenience, it has no bearing whatever either on emotional impulses or sex expression.

Certainly the ritual of marriage has no bearing on the life and habits of human beings. At best, the institution is no more than a public sanction of a private arrangement between two people. Never has the state been able to give more than this sanction, since it will always be love which dominates such human relations.

I often smile at the old references to so-called free love. As though love could ever be anything but free!

Nowadays thousands of people submit to the ceremony of marriage, not because they believe in it, but because it protects them from the vulgar pryings into their private lives.

Marriage the Answer

And so, if you behold me married today you have, therein, the answer—if you care to have one! A marriage does not need to lead to a divorce of one's viewpoint.

The greatest offender against the sanctity of privacy has been the state. Since the reaction ushered in by the World War, the state has relinquished most of its other activities to the exclusive business of holding the individual by the throat.

No longer are freedom of movement or taste possible. Numberless restrictions surround the individual from morn to night. What he eats, drinks, reads, sees, the association he makes, the opinion he hears, and whom he foregathers with, are under constant surveillance. The result is that the individual is constantly with the need of devising methods by which he can escape the tentacles of such intrusions and obstructions.

Necessity Mothers Device

Efforts to thwart from without always create a genius for devising means of escape from within. Thus prohibition has only served to whet the American thirst. Suppression of literary effort has only brought forth ever more revolutionary books. Incidentally, it has increased the intelligent interest in and discussion of the proscribed works.

In the matter of travel, with the everlasting interference of movement imposed by passport and visa, the state forces people to exercise all their craft to break though the Chinese wall built around the whole world since the war. That does not mean, however, that people are necessarily taking the state to their bosom.

The same in a measure holds true of marriage. No one with brains goes on believing that it is made in heaven, or should be made on earth by anyone outside of those immediately concerned, but they go through with the process in the same spirit as one takes out a passport or secures a visa—to obtain breathing space and to protect the privacy of human personality.

■ FEMINISM'S FIGHT NOT IN VAIN

(1926)

NOTE—Emma Goldman's varied career has veered from violent denunciation of America and of marriage to her present position in Montreal, Can., where, as a married woman, she asks to be re-admitted to the United States. There is still another paradoxical phase of her life's development— from her old position of militant feminism she has come to take a coolly critical view of woman suffrage. In this article, the third of a series of five, are presented her opinions, on this subject of abounding interest—written exclusively for NEA Service and *Journal Standard*.

If one bears in mind the sweeping prophecies of the "Woman's Rights" women as to the miracles feminism was going to perform, once woman had the right of suffrage and equality in the professions, one would have to admit that the results of feminism are anything but commensurate with the brave fight made by women for their emancipation.

It is not long ago that we were assured by leading feminists that their creed would purify politics, abolish war, do away with all social evils, and create entirely new relations between the sexes. Today, no intelligent feminist would indulge in such silly talk. They have learned first that agelong abuses cannot be done away with by the casting of a vote.

And what is more important, they have learned that women's economic and social emancipation is closely bound up with the general struggle for human emancipation—that complete independence for man as well as woman will come only with the entire change of our present social structure and a proper and collective worth.

Nevertheless, the heroic struggle made by women for so many years in America and Europe has certainly not been in vain. If she is denied equal remuneration for the work she is doing, she has been able nevertheless to prove that she can make good. There is no profession or trade, not even swimming across the English Channel, which is alien to woman.

Finer Dexterity

Thus I learned while in Germany that women in the metal industry during the war showed finer dexterity in the making of delicate instruments than men. That women during the world cataclysm not only could but did perform the most difficult tasks while the men were bleeding on the battlefield need hardly be emphasized at this late date.

Yes women have made good. No longer will anyone dare to insist that her only place is in the home, to waste her substance as domestic drudge or sex commodity. She has broken through her gilded cage and is now out in the world to take her share of responsibility as well as to demand her right to its achievements.

Advanced American women have done that long before the war, but it is only since then that the women abroad are coming into their own. There are very few "Gretchens," clinging, yielding, obedient and submissive, in Germany today. Nor are women in England learning of life and social conditions by means of secrecy and subterfuge. Openly and frankly do they declare their right to whatever knowledge and experience there is in the world.

And even in France, women, besides the right of love, in which they have claimed mastery, are beginning to appreciate that life is more than idle flirtations, that here are grave social problems which demand the attention of women as well as men. In other words, women the world over have become keenly alive to the need of playing the part in the world's struggle.

Vital in Every Domain

Woman today is perhaps the most vital force in every domain of human thought and endeavor.

Whether it is the devitalizing effect of the horrors of war upon a great many men I do not know. I only know that most men of the professional middle class in Europe have lost their grip on life. They seem to have no faith or idealism left. To use a "Freudian" expression, most men today seem to suffer from an inferiority complex. Or it hurt pride that they can no longer play the brave knight and protect woman from living as dangerously as they themselves have lived?

At any rate, most men seem to be lost, "out of a job," as it were. They do not know what to do with themselves in the presence of their erstwhile inferiors.

Alive, Eager and Active

Not so the women I have met in Europe. They impressed me as completely changed in their physical, mental, spiritual and emotional qualities—a new and virile type of womanhood, much more alive, eager, active and free than men.

Many factors have contributed to create the modern type of woman, the most vital factor being sex solidarity among women. Necessity taught them at an early stage in their struggle that the slave has never been freed by his master and that his emancipation could only be brought about by the spirit of solidarity between his fellow slaves.

So, too, the solidarity of sex among women has, I think, been a tremendous impetus and encouragement in their struggle to assert themselves in their right to their place in the world—their right to be themselves.

■ THE ELEMENT OF SEX IN LIFE

(EXCERPTS)*

Truth will out some day. But in general it is the lie that endures. Truth is naked, straightforward. It will have no smirking, subterfuge or compromise. See lies adorned in silk and jewels. They are smooth, ingratiating and deceptive. The many, all too many, are dazzled by the pomp and self-importance of lies and follow gladly, unaware of the grinning face beneath the fancy mask.

It is, therefore, not surprising that the most elemental force in human life, sex, should still be degraded and denied.

The two institutions that have for centuries tried to subdue sex, to drive it out by the most fiendish methods, have been the church and morality—the traducers of all that is fine and wholesome in life. But the more the church and morality have attempted to subdue sex, burn it out from the needs of man, the more consumingly and devastatingly sex has asserted itself.

It is in comparatively recent years that the truth about sex has broken through the network of falsehood, delusion and snare that has so long haunted man's mind.

----

*Undated. The full manuscript can be consulted in the Emma Goldman Papers of the International Institute of Social History, Ms. 213. It consists of typed notes and quotations, heavily corrected in pencil and not always readable. The excerpts included here are drawn from those portions that were both relevant and legible. The very rough state of the manuscript has necessitated some corrections of spelling, grammar, and punctuation, but only the most necessary changes have been made. —Ed.

And all [the leaders and pioneers in the field of sex psychology] prove beyond a shadow of a doubt that phobias, terrors, neuroses and their mental derangement all have the same sexual origin. More than this, our simplest actions are entirely dependent upon our sexual impulses. The dissimulation imposed by long moral restraint prevented us from recognizing this fundamental truth. But since it is impossible to resist such a powerful natural force with impunity, most people were becoming more or less insane: some were completely so, some expressed their sexual aspirations by transitory phobias or monstrous dreams; others, in order to free themselves from them passed almost their whole existence in a waking dream, indifferent to ordinary life. Finally, those who were strongest satisfied their propensities by the aid of a calculating hypocrisy which enabled them to conceal them from the eye of the crowd.

The growing accumulation of Freudian research, the ever-widening consequences of the application of the original doctrines, supply explanations of many problems which used to puzzle us, and often enable us to find material proof of the theory of the unity of energy: we thus see that dream, sleep, normal state of consciousness and psychoses form an integral part of human personality, which reacts by one or the other of these manifestations to an external influence, according to the actual phase in the evolution of this force. We note that among these forces acting upon us, the most important, if not the only one, which we can almost always find under the most varied disguises, is the sex impulse:

We have to admit that we cannot deny an actual fact, even if we do not like it, and it is therefore indispensible to recognize this much-maligned sex impulse as the great psychological motive force of humanity.

The late Prof. Dorsey, in "Why We Behave Like Human Beings," pointed out that psychology has diagnosed the "impurity complex" and shows us what is back of the blatant prude who advertises his or her "purity." It has also shown that the purity of the ignorant, when purchased at a price of a stifled natural curiosity, is not safe and sane. Prof. Dorsey went on to say that, on the other hand, the study of biology has begun to break down this impurity complex and the unholy, unnatural doctrine begun by early Christian monks that the sex impulse is man's sign of degradation and the source of his most devilish energy. Nature knows better.

Sex is a primary biological function of all life above the lowest. Its characters and qualities have an ancient lineage. Its impulse is as real as is the force which makes the tides to ebb and flow. It has profoundly influenced structure and behavior. It is a fundamental element of all higher life, its external characters a neat advertising dodge of nature by which she sells her wares and thereby insures her family.

To sex we owe more than poetry; we owe the song of birds, all vocal music and the voice itself, the plumage that comes to supreme glory in the bird of paradise, the mane of the lion, the blush of the maiden, the beard of man, and all higher forms of life in plant and animal worlds. It is woven into every fabric of human life and lays its fingers on every custom. To the debit side of the sex account we must charge many silly stupidities and some of the foulest injustices which go to make the thing we call human culture the amazing and variegated mosaic that it is.

We are more enlightened than we were, but we have not yet reached the stage where the mere mention of sex will not provoke someone to respond with a reproach or an insult. Whole blocks on Main Street assume that "sex knowledge" is of questionable propriety, or, at best, to be kept dark in "doctor books;" or regard it as the banal possession of the frankly shameless. As a result, most pseudo-scientific "sex" literature slops over into the emotions and lets facts alone, or presents facts under disguises. Much of it has no biological background or anything of the laws of life, which govern man no less than every living thing. It is fear (sometimes called "reverence") that makes us "let sex alone." It is mock modesty and foolish shame, masquerading under the name "decency," that compels museums to clothe marble fauns and cover Joves and bronze Cupids with plaster-of-Paris fig leaves, often awry or nicked at the corner. Much mawkishness abroad on the question of sex.

Man is "high," animals are "low"—without minds and of course can have no "souls." We have. Ours is a "divine" parentage. Hence art, from Phidian sculpture to sophomoric poem, tends to the greater glory of man: men and women more like goddesses; gods and goddesses glorified men and women.

And so it came about that the commonest thing in nature next to keeping alive became invested with the sanctity of heaven.

All the modern writers on sex have proven that the old notion of sex as beginning with puberty is false. The sex impulse like all our impulses begins at birth and ends with death. Though in opposition to other animals, man cannot interpret his sexual appetites by action before the end of a respectable number of years (a wonderful cause of nervous disorders from which animals faithful to the periodic returns of sexual excitement are free), it nonetheless seems as though there was an awakening of sexuality in him from the earliest days of his life; for Freud and school, sexual ideas come into being the time the child is given the breast.

It seems it is not alone the sensation of the satisfaction of appetite which impels the new-born child to seize the breast of his mother or nurse. In this little shapeless ball, in whom the whole range of sensations has not yet come into being, a special, anticipatory imagination causes the pleasure of satisfied appetites to be already complicated by a more specialized enjoyment.

And late it will be from the earliest years that the child's imagination is turned towards sexual images. Isolated from the world, knowing as yet nothing but family life, already possessed of desires which nature will not allow him to satisfy till a distant future the child will turn his sexual imagination towards the nearest objects, the only ones which he can have in sight. There will be in early infancy an imaginative crisis which will often have a distant reaction upon the sentimental life of the adult.

Psychologists ask us to note:

That the sexual development of the child may take place in three ways:

(1) Appearance of the first phenomena at the very time of birth;

(2) Crisis in later infancy, from four to seven years old, with inversion of normal sentiments, incest, etc;

(3) Crisis of puberty, from about ten to fourteen years of age, followed by a return of the sensations to normal channels.

These psychological manifestations are, no doubt, closely connected with modifications of the internal secretion organs, and, in particular, with sexual development, which is only one department of these glandular activities.

Formerly all these manifestations were met with dense ignorance and stupidity. Over and over again, mothers have whipped and still whip their hapless children when they see the least manifestation of sex. Or they terrorize them and put the stigma of depravity on their children. I could cite hundreds of examples from my own experience as a trained nurse.

Society demands that the young adult man and woman (especially woman) shall repress the sex-impulse for a number of years—often for the whole of their life. The thwarting of such an instinctive urge cannot be achieved in the normal person without interference with health—all sorts of mental and physical disorders may result; and often the impulse, too strong to be thwarted, finds an outlet in some infantile and perverse channel.

In point of truth, many wives dare not give themselves to the uttermost for fear that their husbands would find them too aggressive, lacking in the right kind of femininity. Most men are brought up to believe that woman must be taken and not give herself gladly and joyously in love and passion.

That also prevents the more sensitive of the male species to give themselves freely—they are afraid to outrage and shock the sensibilities and innocence of their wives. You would be surprised how frequent wives do feel shocked and outraged.

Laura, the wife of the captain in Strindberg's "Father," gives us the key to the thoughts and feelings of a great many women. She tells her husband, "When I first came into your life I was like a second mother to you. I loved you like my child. But when the nature of your feelings changed and you appeared as my lover, I blushed and your embrace was joy that was followed by remorseful conscience as if my blood were ashamed." That is the tragedy of many women.

What is commonly called incompatibility of temperaments is nearly always the direct result of lack of sexual harmony—the dissatisfaction and friction which arises when the chemical nature of sex in the man and wife fail to blend harmoniously.

Take frigidity in some women, largely due to the deadening effect of the sex taboo. Such women cannot even if they try desperately respond to the sex urge in the man. In fact, the very thought of the sexual embrace to such women is torture. Even if the man lacks refinement and imposes his needs on his wife, he will find satisfaction. In the end he seeks gratification elsewhere. Sex is more powerful than all decisions. The man will grow indifferent and in the end insist on divorce, or if he can afford it provide for another ménage for his mistress.

Both the Jewish and Christian religions have imposed the notion of the function of sex as only permissible for the act of procreation. That they may be fruitful, multiply, and replenish the earth, Jehovah permitted the Jews to have many wives. The Christian religion, while not permitting many wives and imposing sexual gratification only to bring children into the world, is yet perfectly aware of the fact that whether inside or out of marriage sex is being expressed without much regard to procreation. But while religionists and purists cling to their fetish that sex must not be "indulged" in, as they term the perfectly natural expression, modern biologists and psychologists have torn the veil from all the nonsense pertaining to sex. Whole libraries have been filled with works that treat the subject with understanding and depth and show that there has been an inadequate realization of the tremendous energy back of the sex instinct on the one hand, and, on the other hand, of the biological provisions for the release of this energy along channels not specifically sexual. It is probably absolutely correct to speak of the sex instinct as the creative instinct, and it is equally true that any outlet which offers the emotional satisfaction that comes from creative endeavor has the capability of neutralizing the needs back of the creative craving.

The import of this viewpoint must be fully realized by parents and by their children, for the children reflect them not merely through inheritance, but also by the assimilating of their ideas and ideals. Both must understand and learn to utilize the essentials for developing and satisfying the emotional cravings arising from the sex instinct. It is in this relation that the release of energy along recreational and occupational lines yields the most satisfactory results.

However, the creative spirit is not an antidote to the sex instinct, but a part of its forceful expression. It acts in a conservative manner and utilizes the instinct for forms of satisfaction that are not merely protective in character, but lead on to its greater development, its broadening and deepening in its impress upon innate character and powers of self-direction and control. The non-sexual release of energy sometimes suffices to offset the fundamental needs that lie back of the sexual craving and, in fact, to transmute them into self-satisfying and useful forms of expression.

The man who expressed this thought profoundly and poetically was Friedrich Nietzsche. In "Morality as Anti-Naturalness" he writes: "all passions have a time when they are fatal only, when, with the weight of their folly, they drag their victim down; and they have a later, a very much later, period, when they wed with spirit, when they are 'spiritualized.' Formerly, people waged war against passion itself, on account of the folly involved in it. They conspired for its annihilation. The most notable formula for that view stands in the New Testament, in the sermon on the mount, where, let us say in passing, things are not at all regarded from an elevated point of view. For example, it is there said with application to sexuality, 'If thine eye offend thee, pluck it out.' Fortunately, no Christian acts according to this precept. To annihilate passions and desires merely in order to obviate their folly and its unpleasant results appears to us at present as an acute form of folly. The church fights against passion with excision in every sense, its practice, its 'cure,' its castrations, it never asks, 'how to spiritualize, beautify, and deify a desire?'—it has, at all times, laid the emphasis of discipline upon extermination (of sensuality, of pride, and ambition.)— But to attack the passions at the root means to attack life itself at the root: the praxis of the church is inimical to life ..."

This truism is already recognized by the thinking. But one phase has remained, namely, that sex though a potent factor must not be held in leash by the unmarried.

Fortunately this prejudice too is being demolished. A recent symposium on "the element of sex in the life of the unmarried adult" gives clear and astounding facts of this subject. To quote only a few given by Dr. Ira Wile in his contribution:

> The unmarried possess the potentials of the married group
> to which they are definitely related by interest and partici-
> pation in all the phases of life that affect the well-beings

of the married group. Their sex life, in its various forms, is vital to social welfare, just as it is significant for their own personal growth and development. . . .

Admittedly, to study this phase of sex is to explore one of the uncharted areas of our civilization in which the residua of barbaric ignorance and fear still retard progress. Over its depths appears an uninviting, miasmatic haze of doubt and uncertainty. Few organized explorations have been made of this state of unmarriage. Hence this effort to make a survey of the field from various angles represents an effort to chart facts, to trace causal influences, to determine the validity and worth of current views, and to establish data and hypotheses which may be of service in interpreting our age. . . .

For more than two thousand years the official gratification of procreative urges has been relegated to the socially recognized state of marriage. The assumption of society has been that its authoritative prohibition of the biologic mating urge would postpone its utilization until such a time as the requisite civil or religious rite gave sanction to its usage. If society expected external regulations to subjugate physiologic urges and psychologic impulses, have these regulations been effective? Do those living in unmarriage live in chastity and celibacy? If not, wherein and how do their sexual behaviors differ from those exhibited by fellow beings similar in all else except for living in marriage?

Sexual activity is not an isolated act—it is a general experience motivating and affecting personality. Out of the total personal reaction emerge ideas of romance and beauty, exaltation and peacefulness, devotion and slavish idealization; or, a sense of sacrifice, tumult, humiliation, shame, anxiety, a desire for self-punishment, or a self-accepted weakness, failure and inadequacy.

To interpret the sex life of the unmarried one must recognize that there are two functions of sex:

One, the biologic, which has procreation as a goal—involving some intellectual but more emotional processes in the interest of race preservations.

The other function consists of the promotion of social growth through human relationships. This involves the play function and erotic activity, without or without a procreative goal. There are two bases for the energy of the sexual drive—one, conscious, directed, guided, subjected to ethical controls; the other, unconscious, instinctual, impulsive, reacting to stimuli, but not subject to reason.

Numerous studies have disclosed that the unmarried, like the married, have varied sex experiences. Dr. Klatt found that 18 percent of women had some active form of experience under 18 years. Among Dr. Hamilton's selected professional group, 59 percent of the men and 47 percent of the women had had coitus before marriage, and 20 percent of the males and 16 percent of the females, before 21 years of age. Katherine B. Davis, studying the sex life of 1,200 unmarried college women, reported 61 percent admitting masturbation, of whom 57 percent began before age 15 years.

Sex feelings and desire were experienced with some periodicity in 70 percent of the group reporting on this. The unmarried, no less than the married, reported various forms of sexual phenomena. It is interesting to note that homosexual relations were reported more frequently for the unmarried group. This is significant even though, socially, homosexuality is regarded as more dangerous among men that among women. Much homosexuality among males ceases with confidence in heterosexual potency, as confirmed in mating followed by marriage. . . .

Lesbianism is common and its prevalence is important, though it does not always involve remaining single. The single group regretted the lack of children more than the lack of husbands. Approximately 38.7 percent believed intercourse necessary for complete mental and physical health. Approximately 20 percent justified sexual intercourse before marriage for men and for women.

Dr. Wile asks, "Are the large numbers of adult single undergraduates and graduates of colleges endowed with less sexual drive than high school graduates? Do matured adolescents lose their primary instinctive urges when they become adult? Is higher education purchased at the cost of sexual contraction? This is absurd and contrary to all facts. Sexual activity in one of its many phases exists—whether in active erotic play, auto-erotic, homosexual or heterosexual practice, or as an esthetic or vocational sublimation. Its nature and intensity are subject to personal choice, judgment, standards, and ideals which are regulative but not destructive—temporarily prohibitive rather than permanently inhibitive.

"If one assumes that sexual life is and must be limited by social sanction to those living in wedlock, then what do those living in unmarriage do or what may they do? The question is not what can they do, as this is identical for both groups. The actual legal existence of prenuptial guarantees attests the fact of widespread sexual activity among the unmarried"

Economic inadequacy does not stamp out heterosexual urges any more than the enactment of a punitive law can destroy homosexual impulses. Factually, society recognizes the sexual demands, if not the sexual needs, of the unmarried group in its attitudes toward, and its regulation of, prostitution, homosexual haunts and taxi dance halls.

In other words, the unmarried are either driven to artificial methods of sex expression or they will follow the dominant urge in natural relationships. In point of fact they have done with taboos imposed on them for so long, especially since they have come to know of contracepts to prevent bringing undesired children into this wonderful world of ours—a subject I hope to speak about before I leave your city.

Unmarried adults are approaching sex as a fact rather than a theory. They are accepting their sexual organization frankly as an instrument for personal growth and emotional completion with social stabilization, rather than hypocritically as a function designed by divine plan only for the procreation of pure beings whose excuse for living was that they might die in purity to attain happiness in a world to come.

They appreciate that sex is the source of life, but believe that a sexless life is a mockery after biologic maturation, because it is contrary to nature, since sex is also an expression of psychological factors that socialize individuals and lead them to forsake unmarriage for a marriage in harmony with the laws and customs of their age.

All erotic play is genetically related to courtship, but courtship is subject to social control. Hence, the sex life of the normal young unmarried adult, whatever it may be, is preparation for the perfection of mating the promotion of personal happiness and adjustment in some form of marriage, whether free and unconventional common-law or according to civil or religious rite.

Because I so completely agree with this viewpoint and because I know the disastrous and tragic result of the Puritan idea of sex, I find it imperative to call your attention to the need of treating the sex question frankly and without the subterfuge usually employed when referring to the subject. With the greatest and freest spirits and poet Walt Whitman I say, "Where sex is missing everything is missing." Let us get rid of the mock modesty so prevalent on the surface of polite society. Let us liberate sex from falsehood and degradation and let us realize that sex is a dominant factor for health and harmony in life and in art.

■ SOURCES

"Anarchy and the Sex Question," *The Alarm* 3, no. 3 (September 27, 1896): 3.

"What Is There in Anarchy for Women?" *St. Louis Post-Dispatch* (October 24, 1897).

"The New Woman," *Free Society* (February 13, 1898).

"The Tragedy of Woman's Emancipation," *Mother Earth* 1, no. 1 (March 1906): 9–18.

"The White Slave Traffic," *Mother Earth* 4, no. 11 (January 1910): 344–51.

"Woman Suffrage," *Anarchism and Other Essays* (New York: Mother Earth Publishing Co., 1910): 201–17.

"Marriage and Love," *Anarchism and Other Essays* (New York: Mother Earth Publishing Co., 1910): 233–45.

"The Hypocrisy of Puritanism," *Anarchism and Other Essays* (New York: Mother Earth Publishing Co., 1910): 173–82.

"Mary Wollstonecraft, Her Tragic Life and Her Passionate Struggle for Freedom," (1911) http://theanarchistlibrary. org/library/emma-goldman-mary-wollstonecraft-her-tragic-life-and-her-passionate-struggle-for-freedom.

"Jealousy: Causes and a Possible Cure," (ca. 1912) http://theanarchistlibrary.org/library/ emma-goldman-jealousy-causes-and-a-possible-cure.

"Victims of Morality," *Mother Earth* 8, no. 1 (March 1913): 19–24.

"The Social Aspects of Birth Control," *Mother Earth* 11, no. 2 (April 1916): 468–575.

"Again the Birth Control Agitation," *Mother Earth* 11, no. 9 (November 1916): 669.

"The Woman Suffrage Chameleon," *Mother Earth* 12, no. 3 (May 1917): 78–80.

"Louise Michel," (1923) https://search.socialhistory.org/Record/
ARCH00520.

"Emma's Love Views," *Manitowoc Herald-Times* 29, no. 30
(November 22, 1926): 5.

"Feminism's Fight Not Vain," *Manitowoc Herald-Times* 29, no. 31
(November 23, 1926): 6.

"The Element of Sex in Life," (undated) https://search.
socialhistory.org/Record/ARCH00520.

■ ABOUT THE AUTHOR AND EDITOR

Emma Goldman (1869–1940) emigrated from Russia to the United States in 1885, just as the international anarchist movement was forming, and soon became among the best-known figures associated with anarchism. The remainder of her life was speaking, writing, publishing, and agitating, despite legal harassment, imprisonment, and deportation. Many years after her death, Goldman's ideas remain important influences among both anarchists and feminists. Her works include *Anarchism and Other Essays* (1910), *My Disillusionment in Russia* (1923), and *Living My Life* (1931).

Shawn P. Wilbur is a historian, translator, and curator of the Libertarian Labyrinth digital archive. His published translations include work by Charles Fourier (*The World War of Small Pastries*), Pierre-Joseph Proudhon, and Joseph Déjacque.

ABOUT PM PRESS

PM Press was founded at the end of 2007 by a small collection of folks with decades of publishing, media, and organizing experience. PM Press co-conspirators have published and distributed hundreds of books, pamphlets, CDs, and DVDs. Members of PM have founded enduring book fairs, spearheaded victorious tenant organizing campaigns, and worked closely with bookstores, academic conferences, and even rock bands to deliver political and challenging ideas to all walks of life. We're old enough to know what we're doing and young enough to know what's at stake.

We seek to create radical and stimulating fiction and non-fiction books, pamphlets, T-shirts, visual and audio materials to entertain, educate, and inspire you. We aim to distribute these through every available channel with every available technology—whether that means you are seeing anarchist classics at our bookfair stalls; reading our latest vegan cookbook at the café; downloading geeky fiction e-books; or digging new music and timely videos from our website.

PM Press is always on the lookout for talented and skilled volunteers, artists, activists, and writers to work with. If you have a great idea for a project or can contribute in some way, please get in touch.

PM Press
PO Box 23912
Oakland, CA 94623
www.pmpress.org

FRIENDS OF PM PRESS

These are indisputably momentous times—the financial system is melting down globally and the Empire is stumbling. Now more than ever there is a vital need for radical ideas.

In the years since its founding—and on a mere shoestring—PM Press has risen to the formidable challenge of publishing and distributing knowledge and entertainment for the struggles ahead. With hundreds of releases to date, we have published an impressive and stimulating array of literature, art, music, politics, and culture. Using every available medium, we've succeeded in connecting those hungry for ideas and information to those putting them into practice.

Friends of PM allows you to directly help impact, amplify, and revitalize the discourse and actions of radical writers, filmmakers, and artists. It provides us with a stable foundation from which we can build upon our early successes and provides a much-needed subsidy for the materials that can't necessarily pay their own way. You can help make that happen—and receive every new title automatically delivered to your door once a month—by joining as a Friend of PM Press. And, we'll throw in a free T-shirt when you sign up.

Here are your options (all include a 50% discount on all webstore purchases):

- **$30 a month** Get all books and pamphlets
- **$40 a month** Get all PM Press releases (including CDs and DVDs)
- **$100 a month** Everything plus PM merchandise and free downloads

For those who can't afford $30 or more a month, we have **Sustainer Rates** at $15, $10 and $5. Sustainers get a free PM Press T-shirt and a 50% discount on all purchases from our website.

Your Visa or Mastercard will be billed once a month, until you tell us to stop. Or until our efforts succeed in bringing the revolution around. Or the financial meltdown of Capital makes plastic redundant. Whichever comes first.

Anarchy, Geography, Modernity: Selected Writings of Elisée Reclus

Elisée Reclus
Editors: John P. Clark and
Camille Martin
ISBN: 978-1-60486-429-8
$22.95 • 304 Pages

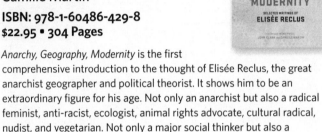

Anarchy, Geography, Modernity is the first comprehensive introduction to the thought of Elisée Reclus, the great anarchist geographer and political theorist. It shows him to be an extraordinary figure for his age. Not only an anarchist but also a radical feminist, anti-racist, ecologist, animal rights advocate, cultural radical, nudist, and vegetarian. Not only a major social thinker but also a dedicated revolutionary.

The work analyzes Reclus' greatest achievement, a sweeping historical and theoretical synthesis recounting the story of the earth and humanity as an epochal struggle between freedom and domination. It presents his groundbreaking critique of all forms of domination: not only capitalism, the state, and authoritarian religion, but also patriarchy, racism, technological domination, and the domination of nature. His crucial insights on the interrelation between personal and small-group transformation, broader cultural change, and large-scale social organization are explored. Reclus' ideas are presented both through detailed exposition and analysis, and in extensive translations of key texts, most appearing in English for the first time.

> "Maintaining an appropriately scholarly style, marked by
> deep background knowledge, nuanced argument, and
> careful qualifications, Clark and Martin nevertheless reveal
> a passionate love for their subject and adopt a stance of
> political engagement that they hope does justice to Reclus'
> own commitments."
> —*Historical Geography*

Revolutionary Women:
A Book of Stencils

Queen of the Neighbourhood

ISBN: 978-1-60486-200-3
$12.00 • 128 pages

A radical feminist history and street art resource for inspired readers! This book combines short biographies with striking and usable stencil images of thirty women— activists, anarchists, feminists, freedom-fighters, and visionaries.

It offers a subversive portrait history which refuses to belittle the military prowess and revolutionary drive of women, whose violent resolves often shatter the archetype of woman-as-nurturer. It is also a celebration of some extremely brave women who have spent their lives fighting for what they believe in and rallying supporters in climates where a woman's authority is never taken as seriously as a man's. The text also shares some of each woman's ideologies, philosophies, struggles, and quiet humanity with quotes from their writings or speeches.

The women featured are: Harriet Tubman, Louise Michel, Vera Zasulich, Emma Goldman, Qiu Jin, Nora Connolly O'Brien, Lucia Sanchez Saornil, Angela Davis, Leila Khaled, Comandante Ramona, Phoolan Devi, Ani Pachen, Anna Mae Aquash, Hannie Schaft, Rosa Luxemburg, Brigitte Mohnhaupt, Lolita Lebron, Djamila Bouhired, Malalai Joya, Vandana Shiva, Olive Morris, Assata Shakur, Sylvia Rivera, Haydée Santamaría, Marie Equi, Mother Jones, Doria Shafik, Ondina Peteani, Whina Cooper, and Lucy Parsons.

> "What an amazing creative way to magnify, and illuminate the courage of 30 Sheroes whose courage, leadership and character is symbolic of the many unsung Women Sheroes of past and present."
>
> —Emory Douglas, Former Black Panther Party Member, Revolutionary Artist & Minister of Culture